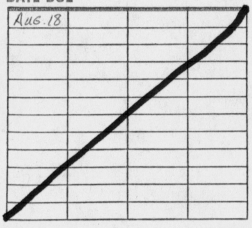

William W. Jellema, Editor

Foreword by
Frederic W. Ness

EFFICIENT
COLLEGE
MANAGEMENT

Jossey-Bass   Publishers
San Francisco • Washington • London • 1973

EFFICIENT COLLEGE MANAGEMENT
William W. Jellema, Editor

Copyright © 1972 by: Jossey-Bass, Inc., Publishers
615 Montgomery Street
San Francisco, California 94111

&

Jossey-Bass Limited
3 Henrietta Street
London WC2E 8LU

Library of Congress Catalogue Card Number LC 73-188135

International Standard Book Number ISBN 0-87589-134-9

Manufactured in the United States of America

JACKET DESIGN BY WILLI BAUM
FIRST EDITION
First printing: May 1972
Second printing: October 1973

Code 7218

The Jossey-Bass
Series in Higher Education

To the administrators in
American colleges and universities—
especially those in the
Association of American Colleges—
this book is dedicated

Foreword

The higher education community has been frequently criticized for failing to observe the principles of effective management, particularly in times of financial stringency. As we look across the broad spectrum of institutions, we would have to recognize some validity in the criticism. But the evidence of interest in improving management, especially in the fiscal area, is unmistakable.

In this spirit, the Board of Directors of the Association of American Colleges agreed that it would be most opportune to devote an annual meeting to this subject. We planned to focus attention upon some of the key areas where improved administrative practices could have a significant effect upon the viability of our colleges and universities. The papers presented at that meeting provided the basis for an exceptionally useful handbook deserving the attention of trustees, administrators, faculty, and in some instances students—in fact, of all who share an interest in improving the quality of the higher education enterprise.

Efficient College Management is a selection of those papers, reedited and, in some instances, substantially rewritten, together with additional material requested by the editor to round out the whole. I hope that this publication will be an important step toward the efficient management of our academic resources.

FREDERIC W. NESS
President
Association of American Colleges

Preface

Two basic steps can be taken to meet a financial pinch: increase income and reduce expenditures. One form of expenditure reduction, however, is sufficiently discrete to warrant separate attention: proper management of available revenue and care in making expenditures—in short, efficient fiscal management. If colleges and universities, public and private, are to prosecute successfully their just case for increased support—especially from state and federal governments—they must also be able to demonstrate to their several constituencies that they are efficient fiscal managers. To aid administrators in their efforts to manage income and expenditures efficiently and to provide them with ready access to some of the ammunition they need in order to persuade others of the importance of efficient management, *Efficient College Management* has been assembled.

There is a limit to the benefits of economizing. Turning off the lights in the White House will not pay for the operations of the Department of Agriculture, let alone the Department of Defense. Similarly, cutting off heat in the hockey area—even if the college has a hockey area—will not redeem the fiscal imbalance in student aid. As Howard Bowen has pointed out, an institution that takes advantage of all current suggestions for increasing efficiency may reduce its budget by no more than 1 per cent.

Quickly, however, one must hasten to say two things. First, 1 per cent of the budget for multimillion-dollar operations is well worth thinking about. Second, if one extends the area for potential efficiency to include the things that Bowen and Gordon Douglass talk about in *Efficient College Management* 1 per cent as an estimate of possible savings may well be much too low. The Bowen-Douglass proposals alone may easily save 5 or 6 per cent of the educational and general budget.

There are still institutions that have left relatively un-cultivated—in terms of fiscal efficiency—some areas of planning and management.

There are still institutions whose investments could be better managed.

There are still institutions that handle their administrative staff organization, development, and evaluation at less than the optimum level.

There are still institutions that do not plan ahead as intelligently as they could—although, in my study of the financial status of private colleges and universities, one of the benefits of the financial crunch most frequently reported by institutions was that it had forced increased attention to long-range planning.

The are still institutions whose faculty members have not yet realized that we must begin to utilize some of the techniques and approaches to instruction that will move higher education from its status as a handicraft industry. We have been like the barber—unable to deal with more than one head at a time.

There are still institutions that have not realized the need for management information systems, efficient handling of admissions, and tight control over intercollegiate athletics.

There are still institutions that have not attained the benefits to be derived from interinstitutional cooperation, that have not been fully imaginative about new sources of income, that have not achieved optimal efficiency in the handling of student services.

Indeed, is there any institution that has done all of these things as well as it could?

Acknowledging the need for better fiscal management

and implementing cost-cutting procedures are two different things. But the time to do both has already arrived for many institutions and is imminent for most others.

Each of the persons preparing a chapter for *Efficient College Management* was asked to concentrate on the fiscal aspects of his management topic but to set it in the context of institutional priorities. Because this is difficult in brief compass, most writers assumed the existence of priorities and concentrated on forwarding them effectively. Warren Bryan Martin rightly challenges this quick formal bow to priorities. Higher education, he says, does not have a sufficiently keen sense of purpose. It is misplaced emphasis to speak of managing efficiently what one does not clearly understand.

This criticism is reminiscent of Robert F. Mager's delightful preface to *Preparing Instructional Objectives.*

> Once upon a time a Sea Horse gathered up his seven pieces of eight and cantered out to find his fortune. Before he had traveled very far he met an Eel, who said, "Psst. Hey, bud. Where 'ya goin'?"
>
> "I'm going out to find my fortune," replied the Sea Horse, proudly.
>
> "You're in luck," said the Eel. "For four pieces of eight you can have this speedy flipper, and then you'll be able to get there a lot faster."
>
> "Gee, that's swell," said the Sea Horse, and paid the money and put on the flipper and slithered off at twice the speed. Soon he came upon a Sponge, who said, "Psst. Hey, bud. Where 'ya goin'?"
>
> "I'm going out to find my fortune," replied the Sea Horse.
>
> "You're in luck," said the Sponge. "For a small fee I will let you have this jet-propelled scooter so that you will be able to travel a lot faster."
>
> So the Sea Horse bought the scooter with his remaining money and went zooming through the sea five times as fast. Soon he came upon a Shark, who said, "Psst. Hey, bud. Where 'ya goin'?"
>
> "I'm going out to find my fortune," replied the Sea Horse.
>
> "You're in luck. If you'll take this short cut," said

the Shark, pointing to his open mouth, "you'll save your-self a lot of time."

"Gee, thanks," said the Sea Horse, and zoomed off into the interior of the Shark, there to be devoured.

The moral of this fable is that if you're not sure where you're going, you're liable to end up someplace else.

If carried too far, however, this criticism begins to develop a marked resemblance to the opinion in some quarters that financial support should be withheld "until higher education gets its house in order." Certainly higher education must change; certainly its institutions must continually clarify their sense and their order of priorities; certainly institutions must be well managed. But the process of educating and support for the process cannot be suspended until refinement is complete.

The chapters that follow are devoted to the fiscal aspects of certain management problems. The topics singled out for attention are among the most critical in contemporary problem areas. Moreover, a great many aspects of the problems other than the fiscal are dealt with in *Efficient College Management*. Teaching is more than productivity; admissions is more than recruitment; collective bargaining is more than contracts; governance is more than its cost of operation; cooperation is more than cutting expenses; and institutional research is more than efficiency. The authors of these chapters know these things. The fiscal aspects of the topics discussed, however, provide the theme that ties these chapters together. Through them all run suggestions for the development of management procedures that will enable each institution to make the most effective use of its resources in order to further its educational objectives.

The chapters in the first part of *Efficient College Management* concentrate on the need for and uses of information. Good management requires systematically organized information, tied to both budgeting and long-range planning. Since even on very small campuses higher education is a multimillion-dollar operation, relatively small errors of judgment can become big dollars of deficit. Coming close is not good enough as an ideal. While the state of the art will not yet entirely take away the worry of being close, it does make it possible to be more accurate than we could be formerly.

The chapters in the second part concern fiscal aspects of intramural and extramural cooperation. Perhaps *cooperation* is much too homely a term to describe what is taking place on some campuses in the areas of governance and collective bargaining. These are, however, contemporary topics in a general discussion of what it means for the constituent elements of the academic community to get along together. Chapter Seven extends the discussion to fiscal aspects of cooperation among institutions.

The third part deals with expenses involved in dealing with students—especially the cost of providing instruction. This item is the major expenditure in the educational and general budget—and it should be. Can the quality of instruction be maintained—or even improved—on less money? Other elements in student costs are the steadily mounting roster of student services which an institution is expected to provide. If an institution cannot afford to offer all services, how does it determine priorities? If it must offer many services, how can it perform them for the least amount of money?

The final part deals more narrowly with private higher education. Many of the problems discussed are not unique to private education, but the examples chosen are those in private institutions; and the problems—admissions, additional sources of income, survival itself—are rather more acute for private than for public colleges and universities.

Here, then, are some of the fiscal aspects of modern management problems as they are set in a context of institutional priorities. They are offered in the belief that while nonfinancial objectives ought to have priority in an academic institution, the financial aspects have a direct bearing on the ability of the institution to perform its academic task. Almost every institution can improve its efficiency of operation.

A number of wonderful people contributed to the assembly of these documents, to all of whom I am grateful.

Washington, D.C.   WILLIAM W. JELLEMA
March 1972

Contents

Contributors

HOWARD R. BOWEN, *chanc⟨dlor, Claremont University Center*

NEIL S. BUCKLEW, *vice-provost, Central Michigan University*

GORDON K. DOUGLASS, *professor and chairman of economics, Pomona College*

G. WAYNE GLICK, *president, Keuka College*

WILLIAM W. JELLEMA, *executive associate and research director, Association of American Colleges*

DENNIS L. JOHNSON, *president, Johnson Associates*

WARREN BRYAN MARTIN, *coordinator of development, University of California, Berkeley*

THOMAS R. MASON, *director of institutional research, University of Colorado*

REXFORD G. MOON, JR., *vice-president and director of studies, Academy for Educational Development*

FREDERIC W. NESS, *president, Association of American Colleges*

ROBERT J. PARDEN, *dean, School of Engineering, University of Santa Clara*

GEORGE B. WEATHERSBY, *associate director, Office of Analytical Studies, University of California, Berkeley*

HERBERT H. WOOD, *president, Kansas City Regional Council for Higher Education*

SHARVY G. UMBECK, *president, Knox College*

Efficient
College
Management

PART I

CONTRIBUTIONS OF PROGRAM BUDGETING AND INSTITUTIONAL RESEARCH

It is by no means certain that having more information will make administrators more comfortable in dealing with fiscal problems. One advantage to having little information is that it provides a ready-made excuse for decisions that turn out badly. More information substantially weakens that excuse without simultaneously guaranteeing that only right decisions will be made. Information must still be interpreted. The Oracle at Delphi and the computer have much in common.

Information may contribute to managerial discomfort in another way: there is often a lot of it. Many an administrator asks what he thinks is a simple question and ends up—like the little girl and the penguins—being told rather more than he cares to learn about that particular subject.

Another problem with information is that it may be admired for its own sake rather than as a means to an end. Management information is not meant to be idle but active. It is chiefly of value not in an academic but in an applied sense. *George B. Weathersby,* an acute observer of the uses to which information is put—or not put—on many campuses, encourages administrators to take courage—and information—and act.

Robert J. Parden discusses the whole program-budgeting process, offering an ordered series of steps that begin with the objectives of the institution, run through the fiscal implications, and return through evaluation to the institution's goals and objectives.

The techniques employed by institutional researchers are especially useful in the conduct of budgetary analyses and cost studies that can result in a more efficiently functioning institution. The budget reflects the priorities of the institution. The role of institutional research, therefore, insists *Thomas R. Mason,* ought to be to evaluate the effectiveness of the use of resources toward the fulfillment of institutional objectives. Without a clear understanding of institutional priorities and a clear statement of institutional objectives, *Warren Bryan Martin* reminds us, institutional research will confirm the obvious or catalog the irrelevant. It clearly has a higher calling.

CHAPTER 1

Purpose, Persuasion, Backbone, and Spunk

George B. Weathersby

Fiscal stringency is the major management problem of higher education today. "Cut, squeeze, and trim!" echoes through hallowed halls more accustomed to open-handed generosity than to public accountability. Our fair-haired boys now sport lengthy locks—to the disgust of parents, voters, and legislators. College presidents are plagued with student unrest, disillusioned faculty, disaffected alumni, and disenchanted donors. Our honeymoon with the public is over. The hundreds of campuses opened in the beginning of the 1950s have entered an age of adolescence characterized by uncoordinated growth, intolerance of academic traditions, spasmodic yet creative experimentation, and a blemished public complexion.

Harried college administrators are, like the Israelites in the wilderness, looking to the tools of modern management to part the seas of red ink that stain their ledgers, hold back the cataclysmic social tides sweeping their campuses, and deliver them safely to the promised land. Unfortunately, by themselves, the tools of modern management, including program budgeting and systems analysis, are hollow forms and faint facades of vicarious leadership.

Leadership versus Management

We often confuse management with leadership—to the detriment of both. Leadership is knowing where to go; management is knowing how to get there. Leadership is setting desirable objectives; management is discovering efficient methods of achieving these objectives. Leadership is charismatic, qualitative, idealistic; management is analytical, quantitative, pragmatic. Managerial tools are reproducible, exportable, and politically demonstrable; leadership is unique, innate, and amorphous.

However, "managers" and "leaders" should not gaze at each other across an unfathomable abyss; indeed, they walk the same road and shoulder complementary responsibilities. The manager asks the leader, What are your objectives? What are your goals? How will you know if you have achieved your objectives? What are the relative values of partial fulfillment of your goals? What items are really important to you? How important? How far into the future are you concerned about your institution? The partial answers to these difficult questions, mixed with institutional data and a knowledge of relevant academic disciplines, form the substance of college and university management. While both leaders and managers can and do exist separately, their catalytic reaction is the energy that powers a dynamic institution. However, this fiducial and mutually reinforcing reaction requires an appropriate supportive atmosphere.

One key indicator of the difference between a leader and a manager is the scope of responsibility and the ways of measuring that responsibility that each perceives. Typically, a leader is concerned with the entirety of his institution and the surrounding community, while a manager is concerned primarily with that narrow margin of institutional resources that are truly discretionary in any one period. A president is concerned with the quality of personal interaction between faculty members, with the professional recognition of his faculty, with the time and resources that students are investing in their education, with the involvement of the community in the life of the campus. Most managers are not concerned with these items because they do not appear in the accounting system; they are not a financial or physical resource of the institution. If the planning process is to be the vehicle of improved leader-manager communication, then program budgeting should be defined by the concerns of the leader, not by the manager's conceptions of resources and expenditures; and activities should be defined by the concerns of the president, not by the traditions of the accountants.

However, it is often very difficult to recognize an institution from its own data. We often forget that the nucleus of most institutions is the relationship between one faculty member and one or more students. A vast superstructure of advisors, committees, and administrators exists to initiate and nurture this relationship. Yet all we can do is count square feet, dollars, and noses—and we are not certain whether they are full-time or part-time noses. We know very little about the cognitive or affective changes in students or faculty attributable to their interaction in an institution.

The incongruence of the manager's data system (space, dollars, and people) with the leader's planning concerns (relationships, experiences, intellectual and attitudinal development) can inhibit communication and drastically reduce their mutual effectiveness. If, however, academic, fiscal, and physical planning in an institution can be integrated, relevant policy analysis is facilitated. A Planning, Programing, Budgeting System (PPBS) attempts to integrate all institutional resource commitments into a single display and thus to coordinate intermediate and long-range institutional planning.[1]

[1] For a review of PPBS in postsecondary education see F. E. Balderston and G. B. Weathersby, "PPBS in Higher Education Planning and Management (A Three Part Series)," *Higher Education*, 1972, *1* (2, 3, 4); and J. Farmer, *Why Planning, Programming, Budgeting Systems for Higher Education?* (Boulder: Western Interstate Commission for Higher Education, 1970.)

Another key indicator of the difference between a leader and a manager is the attitude of each toward program costs. Managers generally look upon such costs as *facts;* leaders regard them as *opinions.* In the view of many managers, resources have precise costs. A ream of paper costs $1.82; an assistant professor, Step III, costs $11,400 plus 10 per cent for fringe benefits; a laboratory retort costs $17.23—no more, no less. But how much does a new doctoral program in environmental studies cost? While the direct faculty and support costs may seem obvious, should a portion of the costs of the library, the admissions office, the health service, the telephone system, and the president's secretary be allocated? To maximize overhead recovery from an extramural source of funds, an institution prefers to allocate all these costs; yet in making a decision on the new doctoral program, one probably should not allocate any of them. Thus, the cost of a program does not correspond to the precise costs of its resources. In other words, program costs are opinions, not facts. What about the costs of administrative decisions? Now we return to the world of facts because no prorations are involved. If a dean desires to hire a new professor and increases his departmental allocations by twenty thousand dollars, this decision clearly costs the institution twenty thousand dollars. Resource costs and decision costs are determined by the economic marketplace, while program costs are determined by the judgment of an administrator or an analyst.

Use of Quantitative Analysis and PPBS

If program costs are not facts but opinions, if our entire structure of institutional data serves managers and not leaders, if a manager's perspective is but a small subset of a leader's world view, then how can management tools and approaches be of value to leaders?

In the first place, even though educational objectives rarely are clearly known and accurately articulated, quantitative analysis may still be of assistance. As Hitch points out: "Learning about objectives is one of the chief objects of this kind of analysis. We must learn to look at objectives as critically and as professionally as we look at our models and our other inputs. We may, of course, begin with tentative objectives, but we must expect to modify or replace them as we learn about the systems we are studying—and related systems. The feedback on objectives may in some cases be the most important result of our study." [2] Quade comments on the contributions of managers and leaders in the formulating of objectives: "Objectives are not, in fact, agreed upon. The choice, while ostensibly between alternatives (management), is really between objectives or ends, and nonanalytic methods (leadership) must be used for a final reconciliation of views." [3]

Unlike the traditional administrative functions of accounting and inventory control, program budgeting and systematic analysis question institutional objectives, probe the purposes of institutional activities, and engage the president in dialogue designed to assess the practical and political feasibility of stated institutional objectives. This is why PPBS poses a direct challenge to the general decision-making machinery of government (and education).[4] This is also why an honest fiducial relationship between leader and management analyst is essential.

Ideally, program budgeting arrays all the capital and operations costs associated with the orchestrating of personnel, equipment, facilities, and all other resources in the achievement of a specific, quantified objective of the organization. Even if the objectives are neither specific nor quantified, program budgeting still enables a decision maker to examine the total costs occurring both now and in the foreseeable future for comparable alternatives. If the analysis includes political and social costs and benefits, in addition to the usual economic

---

[2] C. J. Hitch, *On the Choice of Objectives in System Studies* (Santa Monica, Calif.: RAND, 1960), p. 19.

[3] E. S. Quade, *Analysis for Military Decisions* (Chicago: Rand McNally, 1964), p. 176.

[4] A. Wildavsky, "The Political Economy of Efficiency: Cost-Benefit Analysis, Systems Analysis, and Program Budgeting," *Public Administration Review,* 1966, *26*(4), p. 302.

costs and benefits, then the decision maker has most of the information he needs to choose one of the alternatives.

However, quantified, systematic analysis goes one step further: it generates new and better alternatives. While program budgeting enables a leader to compare various alternative policies, the generation of new policy alternatives (structured by the framework of the program classifications) is left to the imagination and creativity of the analyst. With a fully articulated description of the way the relevant components of the educational system interrelate, however, the decision maker can synthesize new alternatives analytically—and each new alternative is guaranteed to be better than the previous alternative. This ability alone is a powerful and persuasive argument for the serious consideration of and experimentation with systematic analysis and program budgeting.

Although systematic analysis has no easy answers for the problems confronting educational administrators, it does offer several approaches and possibilities that *may* alleviate internal conflict. For example, there may be either pervasive agreement or violent discord on an issue as broad as "meaningful undergraduate education." However, when "undergraduate education" is decomposed into various skills, experiences, choices, proficiencies, and other attributes, we can begin both to isolate areas of major conflict and to identify areas of widespread agreement. In the areas of conflict, educational leaders can seek new, imaginative alternatives (such as new colleges or work-study plans) acceptable to all the interested parties, or conflicting groups can learn to coexist (as in experimental ungraded courses and separate black studies programs). At least, administrators can draw an unambiguous line of demarcation around the issues of conflict so that they may preserve as much as possible of the mutually accepted and treasured ethos of the institution.

Another possibility for the amelioration of conflict lies in the decentralization of decision making from a system, say, to an individual campus or department. Local administrators can then concentrate on outputs of the educational process rather than inputs, and individual students and faculty members can select institutions on the basis of specific goals served and rewarded by the institution (such as undergraduate liberal-arts instruction or graduate instruction in the sciences). Resources could be allocated to a campus or an institution by a central administrator according to the degree to which that campus satisfies its objectives and according to the relative value placed upon its overall objectives by the funding agency. This manner of resource allocation would enable, though not require, each institution to develop its own character, provide greater diversity in a system or state, and reduce the scope of consensus required for a decision. All these factors should lead to at least a partial resolution of conflicting goals, objectives, and values.

Other conflict-resolution mechanisms exist in systematic analysis and program budgeting. Most important, however, the quantitative articulation of problems of resource allocation provides a structure for the communication of values and objectives, and for the decomposition of complex, convoluted problems into smaller, more manageable problems. Thus, the various segments of the constituency of an institution are given a vocabulary with which to explore their areas of agreement and seek resolution of their remaining differences. However, as we suggested previously, this analytical approach requires nurture and development, and opportunity for the protagonists to learn how to relate to one another within this structure.

Conclusions

Confronted with complex, expensive educational organizations, institutional leaders and managers have begun to turn to PPBS and the analytical tools of modern management for assistance. These quantitative techniques have the potential to rationalize institutional planning processes; to provide a communication link between leaders and managers, between students and faculty, between administrators and staff; to stimulate an intellectual climate of debate and discussion on central issues; and ultimately to allocate scarce human, physical, and fiscal resources in a more efficacious manner.

However, none of the available quantitative tools or models addresses all the problems confronting college presidents today, and none of them addresses these pressing problems as thoroughly or as forcefully as it could. Why not? One reason is that analysis costs money, and in the short run it costs more money than not doing analysis at all. Given this condition, we almost always prefer to repeat yesterday's mistakes than to avert tomorrow's disasters. Another reason is that educational administrators do not really know either what to expect and to demand from quantitative analysts or how to respond to the demands of their analysts. In other words, the necessary mutual understanding and fiducial relationship does not exist. A third reason is that analysis runs counter to many long-established academic traditions. Academia has about as many sacred cows as all of ancient India, and traditional analysts face a similar number of untouchable subjects. Furthermore, current administrators feel threatened by these old concepts cloaked in new words and implemented on computers.

Despite these understandable rationalizations, today's problems—student unrest, increasing political pressures, flagging financial and moral support, increasing environmental concern—demand more than tired excuses based upon short-sighted economy, inadequate awareness of administrators, and staid tradition. Public accountability requires, and a bureaucratic sense of self-preservation demands, a vigorous, positive, convincing response to these problems. The most vigorous, positive, and convincing response available is a dynamic leader cognizant of and committed to the spirit and techniques of modern management and embued with another PPBS: Purpose, Persuasion, Backbone, and Spunk.

CHAPTER 2

Planning, Programming, and Budgeting Systems

Robert J. Parden

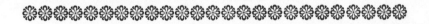

The tendency is strong in most universities to expand in more directions than available finances make wise. The resulting poverty is shared by all. These words of Joseph Willits and Malcolm Preston suggest why program budgeting should be of interest to all colleges and universities.

Contemporary college and university budgeting procedures evolved in support of the accounting functions—authorization, control, and accountability. These needs continue. Program budgeting adds a cost-benefit dimension to aid in planning and allocation decisions.

Program budgeting is a special case of systems analysis. The university and its environment form a system. Each activity or program is considered not only by itself but also in relation to all the other activities that make up the university.

11

In other words, when a decision is to be made, the "total picture" is considered.

The heart of program budgeting is the grouping of activities by programs whose resources and costs can be assessed and whose benefits or contribution to the institution can be identified. The appropriate program size is one that is sufficiently precise to allow review as an entity but not so small as to create an unmanageable listing of activities.

Program-Budgeting Cycle

Ten steps can be used to describe the process of program budgeting.

First, *establish goals and objectives.* Program budgeting uses the goals of an institution as a basis for comparing alternate programs. The programs that appear to satisfy the goals best and are within available resources are chosen. Objectives are goals translated into numerical levels of achievement. Translation into numerical terms reduces dispute about degree of goal achievement. This step is directly related to the evaluation phase (step 8). Without agreement on both the goals and the manner of measuring achievement, the evaluation step is meaningless.

Second, *develop alternate programs that will accomplish the same goals.* The number of degree programs offered, the degree level provided, the combination of large or small sections, high or low faculty-student ratios, the degree of involvement in sponsored research—these are but a few of the alternates from which an institution must select in developing the strategy by which it reaches its goals and objectives.

An institution can reach its goals by various routes. It may, for instance, choose to play a unique role in higher education. (The resource implications of this uniqueness should be clearly understood.) Or it may select a reasonably standard program and develop a unique environment for presentation. (This approach may have a greater impact than an inadequately supported uniqueness.) Again, the institution may select one portion of the total spectrum of activity and, by emphasizing that part, free others to make other contributions. The freedom to select new roles lessens as an institution develops facilities, faculty, and competence in any one area. This built-in commitment creates an inertia that is difficult to reverse if the benefits of the program decline. Therefore, the long-range resource impact of all program proposals should be carefully developed.

One of the most difficult phases of the program-budgeting procedure is to encourage the development and implementation of truly unique and meaningful educational experiments. Concern for academic programs may become secondary to administrative functions unless there is constant effort to refocus on the central purpose of the university. This is not unique to program budgeting. In a program-budgeting system, however, all programs become visible. This may encourage the development of new approaches, especially when it is made clear that new programs have a competitive chance.

Third, *estimate resource requirements for each alternative.* The term *resource* is used to describe all the support that a program requires. Resources include salaries, space, supplies, equipment, and all other needs translated into their dollar equivalents. The simplest resource calculations are those related to classroom teaching. If there is a standard faculty teaching load, the salary of the full-time faculty member can be readily allocated to each of his activities. By totaling all the students enrolled in each course and dividing this total into the faculty costs, one can easily calculate a faculty teaching cost per student credit hour. To this base can be allocated all the departmental costs, counseling, administration, equipment, and clerical expense. There may be an overemphasis on the calculation of unit costs for courses because the data are readily available.

Program budgeting encourages the identification and retention of activities whose costs as well as benefits are accumulated—a counseling service operated by the dean of students, for example. If its costs are arbitrarily allocated to the instructional departments via student credit hours, it loses its identity for evaluation as a program. Unit-cost calculations and program-resource implications may use the same data but do not serve the same purpose.

Fourth, *estimate benefits to be gained from each program alternative.* The identification of program benefits is the most difficult step in the program-budgeting procedure. The impact of a man's education can be seen relative to what he accomplishes in a lifetime, but this impact is difficult to relate to any one campus activity. This difficulty does not mean that we must abandon the program concept and cost-benefit analysis but rather that additional effort must be directed toward identification of benefits. Initially we must accept as measures of output any quantifiable evidence that holds promise of demonstrating that a program will ultimately accomplish the objectives for which it is designed.

Fifth, *develop an operating plan by selecting from among alternatives.* This step involves selecting the combination of programs that best satisfies institutional objectives and goals within the resources available. One way of visualizing this procedure is to think of the process as being undertaken by a single person, perhaps the president (although a decision maker can be anyone—one person, the consensus of a committee, or even a referendum of all participants—who must ultimately choose from among a number of alternatives). He has 1,200 sheets of paper. These include alternatives A, B, and C for each of 400 programs. One of the programs is undergraduate scholarship assistance. Alternative A will support two hundred students and cost $160,000 out of university funds. Alternative B will support three hundred students and cost $210,000. Alternative C will support five hundred students at a cost of $50,000. The more money spent on scholarships, the more the tuition needs to be raised next year for all students. Each alternative therefore represents a different cost, affects different numbers of students, and will have a different impact on the university.

The decision maker can place any one of the alternative scholarship programs at any priority level he wishes among the four hundred programs to be ranked. The priority ranking can be changed as each of the alternatives is reviewed. He must rank programs by goal satisfaction and also by resources required. Each time he considers the next program alternative, he can either add it to the list of programs to be undertaken or use the equivalent resources to enrich one of the programs already given a priority ranking. When he is finished, he may have two or three hundred programs ranked in order of anticipated benefits, using alternative A for some, B or C for others, with their total cost falling within the resources available.

Sixth, *test the long-range fiscal implication of the plan.* There are few decisions made about "one-time-only" resource allocations. Most decisions affect the institution tomorrow and the next day and next year for an indefinite period. So that the long-range implications of each selected alternative program can be seen, a budget for each year during the next five to ten years is compiled. Each time a decision is made about a resource allocation, its impact on future budgets is recorded. For instance, there may have been enough funds to initiate program Y last year and project X this year; but there may not be enough funds next year to let both projects grow at the rate necessary for both to reach a viable level.

The term *simulation* is used to describe compilation of annual budgets, perhaps ten years into the future, by means of a computer. The purpose of simulation is to try various operation strategies. It is possible to vary the values of the factors that influence budgets—for instance, enrollment, tuition, other income, faculty-student ratio, average faculty salaries —to see how the variations would affect the ten-year plan for the university. If, for example, enrollment is raised by two hundred students, tuition income would increase and the number of required faculty would increase. Faculty salaries and other expenses also would increase. How would these increases affect the overall budget?

It is possible to extend these projections by hand. As the model becomes more sophisticated, however, manual calculations become laborious. The computer allows a more rapid calculation as new values for different income and expense categories are tried.

Seventh, *compile the annual budget.* The reason for testing the long-range fiscal implications of the selected alternatives is to pick a combination that will match programs with resources in the immediate future. If five- to ten-year projections indicate the feasibility of undertaking the programs selected, then the first year of the long-range plan can become next year's operating budget. It may require translation into organizational unit allocations, but the planning totals should equal the operating budget totals. The planning activity continues to probe ten years into the future, adding increased precision as the year draws closer. Finally, the projection becomes the operating budget.

Eighth, *evaluate the success of the program.* To evaluate is to measure whether a program as perceived accomplished its goals.

> After you switched to speed-reading techniques, were the third graders able to read faster, comprehend more, retain knowledge longer, as the experimental design suggested?
> No, but . . .

Faculty evaluation by students, course evaluation by alumni, students' evaluation of their environment, measured achievements in cost reduction—all are capable of evaluation by numerical levels of achievement. If the evaluation proves that the goals of the program are not being attained, then other programs should be developed.

Ninth, *revise planning standards.* The process of planning, programming, budgeting, and evaluation is a continuous one. The projected costs and benefits of proposed alternative programs must be assessed as carefully as possible. A standard data file will have to be developed for each institution so that it can predict the consequences of its actions. Initially, the institution may have to estimate values or borrow them from others; but the experience gained by evaluating those programs that have been undertaken can be used to update and refine the data file. For example, an institution may estimate that it needs one full-time secretary for every ten full-time faculty members. This becomes the "standard." If the work does not get out, however, the standard needs to be revised in the light of experience.

Tenth, *repeat the cycle* to accommodate changes in objectives, goals, available resources, and the institution's environment. Ideally, every time a decision is made that influences any program—be it a commitment to expend resources or a change in anticipated income—the information would be used to update the long-range plans and projections of the institution. If the plan is not kept current, it cannot serve a useful purpose in the ongoing, day-by-day decision making.

How may this updating be translated into a working procedure? (1) The procedure will vary with the size of the institution and the formality of its planning activity. If responsibility for long-range planning is assigned to one individual, updating is his responsibility. (2) The planning activity will normally receive all reports on enrollment, finances, and the other statistics necessary to maintain valid long-range projections. (3) There must be formally established lines of communication, so that decisions that affect planning are relayed to the planning activity for interpretation and recording. This communication is most difficult with nonquantified information, items not normally included in operating reports. (4) The compilation of the annual budget is an automatic due date requiring that the long-range plan for the next year be ready to translate into an operating budget. (5) If a long-range planning committee meets on a fixed schedule, this will trigger the frequency with which updating must occur.

Impact of Program Budgeting

A self-study is a comprehensive, introspective analysis of an institution: where it has been, where it is now, where it would like to be. A "master plan," the normal end product of a self-study, is a good way to initiate program budgeting. After that, the process will be a continuous one.

Program budgeting proposes that the costs and benefits of every program be compared with those of every other program on a continuing basis. An existing program does not automatically have priority over all new proposals. At most institutions, this possible threat to existing programs will contribute significantly to resistance to adoption of program budgeting.

Resistance to program budgeting also will be offered on the basis that benefit analysis is too difficult. However, there is no evidence that a lack of analysis is preferable. In any case, no one underestimates the difficulty of assessing the benefits of a particular program. The consequences of one choice in preference to another are often evasive. These nuances are the dimension that the decision maker contributes. Program budgeting requires only that the best possible assessment of benefits be attempted.

Some administrators will resist using program budgeting as a systematic approach to problem solution. As long as they can "play it by ear," their mistakes are more easily rationalized. As situations grow more complex, however, any assistance will be of value.

Program budgeting is not an activity limited to universities with a large computer and a substantial staff for analytical studies. The procedure can be geared to the size of the institution because the smaller unit generally has a less complex operation and considerably shorter lines of communication. The program-budgeting procedure will prove equally informative to the smaller institution.

Currently, management information systems in support of decision making are being developed. In fact, these systems probably will be developed long before there is comparable understanding of the decision-making process in colleges and universities. A management information system supplies the information necessary to support program budgeting as well as day-to-day operations. Management information systems should not be developed before optimal operational systems and procedures are developed and recorded. Few institutions have the patience to wait. Therefore, because the cost of reprogramming changing procedures is rarely anticipated, the cost of implementing data-processing installations has been extremely high.

Finally, there are diminishing returns to program budgeting. The cost of management information systems is considerable. An analytical staff may do analysis with no one listening. Decision makers and the staff who work in support of the decision-making functions must develop a sustained communication. The decision maker cannot abdicate his responsibility to the staff members. The staff assistance must be pertinent, helpful, and timely. There is a need to arrive at reasonable levels of data collection and analysis and to ensure that the information provided is making a genuine contribution to university decision-making. Without this contribution to more effective management, it will not become a justifiable university activity.

CHAPTER 3

Institutional Priorities

Warren Bryan Martin

Gollege and university research units should be crucial instruments for the determination of institutional priorities and management objectives. In fact, however, they are likely to be of minimal usefulness in these areas—not because of professional inadequacies in personnel or the so-called primitive state of the art, but because research must always have both purpose and perspective, and today's institutions of higher education are dissatisfied with practices of the past, ambiguous about existing purposes, and devoid of perspectives appropriate for the future. Research units in these institutions, therefore, must function without an ideational tradition, without a valid context in which to work, and without guidelines by which to plan ahead.

No wonder institutional research confines itself to confirming the obvious or cataloging the irrelevant. Given no better job to do, it does the job it is given. And whatever intellectual capital these offices can muster is then invested in debates such as the one now raging between those authorities on research and planning who would make the IR office on campus the single unit for conducting institutional studies and those authorities who conceive of the IR office as primarily an instigating and coordinating agency for the development of research activities throughout the campus. Should IR itself do all necessary studies, or should the action be decentralized?

Both camps share the fallacious assumption that valid criteria exist for evaluating *any* outcomes. Or perhaps they fear that no answer can be given to the criterion question and that therefore researchers must confine themselves, under one format or another, to studies of time, place, and manner. (How often, as Ramsey's maxim puts it, chronic philosophical disputes rest on mistaken assumptions shared equally by the contending parties.) It is such false assumptions that must be exposed, and it is this escape into gate tending and bookkeeping that must be ended.

Since administrators and faculty can no longer speak with confidence or consensus about the assumptions or values behind educational programs, they content themselves with talk of quantifiable details, existing practices, and procedural innovations. Educators thus may be likened to those churchmen who, having given up on ever gaining agreement on Christian doctrine, decide that they can at least worship together—hoping that preachers who pray together will stay together, no matter what they say or how they say it or to whom their prayers are directed. A shared liturgy gives the appearance of legitimacy. Anyway, better to light a candle than to curse the darkness. So it is said.

But that cliché has a fatal flaw. It is not better to light a candle to dispel the darkness when a deadly enemy is lurking in the shadows. To illuminate your candle, if you are the target, is a sure way to get your candle blown out—or your head blown off. Today, institutional research, together with all of education, has such an enemy. It is not a special-interest group or some conspiratorial subversive element. It is, rather, the criterion demon. Institutional research offices collect data and complete reports that are intended to illuminate, but what they produce does little to push back the darkness or to dispatch that enemy in the shadows.

Here is another illustration of our situation, drawn not from the institutional level but from the federal scene. The National Center for Educational Communication (NCEC) is committed, according to that agency's literature, to five major objectives: to accelerate the spread of exemplary programs and validated practices, to develop communication linkages for effective application of knowledge and improved practices, to assure access to current educational knowledge, to disseminate interpreted information on priority educational topics, and to develop and articulate Office of Education communication efforts. All of these objectives are laudable and could be taken, with minor revisions, as objectives for any institutional research center. But if we ask about the basis for determining "exemplary programs" or the criteria employed in judging "improved practices" or setting "priority educational topics," the answers show that these determinations are made by educational consulting firms working under contract or by the current coterie of policymakers in the executive branch of the government, in USOE, or in the Bureau of the Budget. Such answers are no answers to the question about criteria. They simply refer it along the corridors of the bureaucracy. They do, however, give clues to the criteria actually employed.

The fundamental assumptions or ideational criteria that have motivated and provided the basis for judgments of educational research in the recent past have been those of straight-arrow Western liberalism: confidence in the abilities, worth, and essential goodness of man; emphasis on the individual rather than the community; lip service to democratic processes, tolerance, diversity, pluralism; a preference for education defined as "cognitive rationality" (which means that one prefers coming to the emotions by the mind instead of coming to the mind by the emotions). Furthermore, themes of human development, or organization theory, or educational philosophy are usually unexamined by researchers even as they are poorly articulated, if at all, by those who commission institutional research. Good research does illuminate reality, but what is less evident and equally important is that research also illuminates the researcher's values and those of the sponsoring agency.

Thus, we must qualify our claim about the paucity of theoretical conceptualizations and the absence of broad institutional purposes that serve a coherent cultural rationale. Research does operate from theories and for purposes, but educators have not been sufficiently self-conscious about them until recently. And now—as the truth emerges, as our limp liberal commitments are exposed—we employ the tactic of diversion by pointing to the contributions IR has made and can make in providing demographic information on students; arranging comparative data with institutions of similar size on a wide range of quantifiable measures; presenting, through a review of the literature or by model building, sets of alternative courses of action, curriculum options, innovations, and experiments; and projecting trends or potential consequences of trends.

Some educational research has had value. A considerable body of literature dealing with personality theory has been produced. That students change in values and attitudes as they proceed through the college years has been documented. Information on space utilization has been provided. There is still, however, no comparable body of research literature dealing with intellectual and cognitive change.[1]

All of this, however, is ancillary to our point. Today, as never before, researchers are confronted by contending theories of psychological development or by a revival of that long-standing dispute between behavioral scientists and more humanistically oriented scholars on the comparative significance of the environment in determining individual characteristics (Do institutions shape men more than individuals shape institutions?); at the same time, researchers are devoid of shared assumptions, values, or attitudes. There is no agreement across the methodological lines on the good, the true, and the beautiful.

Today's dogma requires the repudiation of dogma. As a consequence, we are like the foolish professor, in that remark-

---

[1] J. A. Axelrod et al., *Search for Relevance* (San Francisco: Jossey-Bass, 1969).

able thriller entitled *We Still Kill the Old Way,* who innocently tries to solve a crime in a land where there is no justice. How can educational research have widespread consequences when nobody has criteria that engender widespread confidence? Today, there is no agreement on educational philosophy; standard tests and measures contain class or race bias; grading and testing procedures change as often and vary as much as women's fashions; there is no agreement on methods of teaching or means of learning, except perhaps that there is no best way; and the primacy of rationality, the "data fixation" [2] of research methodology, the authority of professionalism, the legitimacy of tenure, the meaning of academic freedom, the representativeness of institutional governance, the socialization goals of postsecondary education—all these traditional benchmarks are disputed if not abandoned. What chance, then, is there for research to do more than confirm biases or prejudices previously agreed upon?

Research Subordinated to Other Interests

Educational researchers are in bad repute not only because of ideational confusion within the institution of higher education, as in the society at large, but also because they have been unable to transcend human subjectivism. They, and other academics, have espoused objectivity, even claimed it; at the same time, they have brought an expanding technology into the service of self-interest. There is enough jealousy, competitiveness, and pettiness among researchers—resulting in conflicting claims—to compel the conclusion that research, like philosophy, is a way men rationalize their passions. The final proof that

[2] See Kenneth Boulding, "Evidences for an Administrative Science," *Administrative Science Quarterly,* 1958, *3*(1), 16–17. Boulding characterizes "data fixation" as follows: "Its principal symptom is a certain obsessiveness with arithmetic—the feeling that once a number has been arrived at by recognized statistical ritual something has been accomplished. . . . I must confess that I regard the invention of statistical pseudo-quantities like the coefficient of correlation as one of the minor intellectual disasters of our time; it has provided legions of students and investigators with opportunities to substitute arithmetic for thought on a grand scale."

education may be futile as a civilizing force lies in the machinations of academics. Despite their commitment to reason, they, hardly less than other human beings, are creatures of emotion.

When professional researchers are not spending time protecting their favorite methodology, instruments, or programs, they are busy prostituting themselves to funding agents or institutional superiors. Allowed neither creativity nor criticism, institutional researchers give back "findings" that support the expectations of their benefactors. Griffiths, speaking about research on educational administration, develops this point and makes two recommendations.

> One of the practices which is most damaging to the reputation of administrative research is engaged in by a large number of professional organizations, state education departments, and school systems. This is the practice of subordinating research to policy development. What happens is this: An organization, say a state education association, is confronted with a problem such as the legislature's considering a bill advocating compulsory merit rating for teachers. The association, through its board of directors, publicly goes on record as opposing the bill while indicating that its research division will "study" the problem. What it actually means is that its research division will dig up the evidence to support its stand.
>
> . . . this sort of practice cannot be continued if research is to command a position of respectability in the educational world. Two steps must be taken if respectability is to be attained. The first step is that administrators must be convinced that research should take place *before* policies are formulated, not afterward; and the second step is that researchers must be taught not to prostitute their labors to the whims of their administrators. Neither of these steps can be attained easily, but attained they must be or administrative research will continue to have little value in the actual administration of organizations.[3]

[3] Daniel E. Griffiths, "Research and Theory in Educational Administration." In *Perspectives on Educational Administration and the Behavioral Sciences* (Eugene, Oregon: Center for the Advanced Study of Educational Administration, 1968), p. 45.

A passage in Shakespeare can stand as a metaphor for the limitless adaptability of most institutional researchers. Says Hamlet, "Do you see yonder cloud that's almost in shape of a camel?" Replies Polonius, "By the mass, and 'tis like a camel indeed." Hamlet again: "Methinks it is like a weasel." Polonius: "It is backed like a weasel." Hamlet: "Or like a whale?" Polonius: "Very like a whale." How often researchers, on command, see in one collection of data a camel, a weasel, a whale.

Research as Cure for Nonconformity

There is disquietude in academe these days over the fact that, as a recent Carnegie Commission report puts it, American colleges are becoming more and more uniform in purposes and procedures.[4] The standardization movement, which has been the chief contributor to institutional conformity, is now over sixty years old. This movement was conceived to put an end to manifold abuses in the packaging and selling of educational programs. And it has been generally effective in doing so. But the guidelines set down became laws, enforced externally by accrediting associations and monitored internally by institutional research offices. The credit system was one offspring of the standardization movement, and its corollaries—hours of credit, FTEs, degrees granted for dollars spent—have been the currency that IR functionaries flash at the administrative bar of justice, as vouchers for their drinks, as justifications for their presence.

Worse is the fact that researchers contributed to a standardization encouraging uniformity and culminating in conformity by taking upon themselves, or sometimes being taken into, the shoddy business of making everybody over in the image of the style setters and lawgivers. IR has helped to put higher education into that one-model box from which, perhaps

---

[4] Harold Hodgkinson, *Institutions in Transition* (Berkeley, Calif.: Carnegie Commission on Higher Education, 1970). See also Warren Bryan Martin, *Conformity: Standards and Change in Higher Education* (San Francisco: Jossey-Bass, 1969).

too late, it is now desperately trying to extricate itself. As long ago as 1931, Samuel P. Capen warned that the standardization movement, however justified at its beginnings, was becoming legalistic and censorious.[5] Capen insisted that evaluation should concern itself exclusively with the intellectual achievement of individuals and with truly educational standards; that educational standards should not be equated with time allocations, organizational hierarchies, and bureaucratic efficiency. We know that today there is no agreement even on educational standards —Capen sounds naïve on this point; but he has been proved right in warning us that researchers, like most educators, are "incorrigibly meddlesome people. Minding somebody else's business has an irresistible attraction for us. And we abhor nonconformity" (p. 4).

Norms for Judgment

What then can be done? Are we to conclude that research has no contributions to make? Some authorities are still sanguine concerning prospects. Paul Dressel, in an essay entitled "The Problems of Evaluation," speaks about several gradations of research. One is summative research, said to be valuable in appraising the overall effectiveness of a program. Then there is formative research, which is evaluation carried on as an aid to development of some program. Another way of approaching institutional research tasks, according to Dressel, is to think of them in conjunction with the prepositions *to, for,* and *with:*

> Evaluation *done to* implies the collection of evidence followed by summative appraisal by persons external to rather than involved in a program. . . . Evaluation *done for* is some improvement in that this may involve a request for the evaluation, and certainly a recognition that the evaluation is necessary, desirable, and ultimately beneficial. . . . When evaluation is *done with,* it becomes a

[5] Samuel P. Capen, "The Principles Which Should Govern Standards and Accrediting Practices," Address to the North Central Association, Chicago, March 18, 1931.

cooperative endeavor involving students, faculty, and evaluators and has continuing interaction with the program in a *formative* mode. . . . Evaluation is then a continuing process—an essential component of the program —rather than an occasional and incidental feature.[6]

Without questioning these concepts of evaluation, or the ability of some of them to elicit potentially useful information (particularly when emphasis is placed on research, development, and evaluation as continuing processes), we still question whether there are any accepted norms for judging institutional research, that research which may be called "disciplined inquiry." Our answer is that there are no such norms—either within the institution or outside.

The public clamors for accountability. Research cannot help in this area until there is some measure of agreement about that toward which educational institutions are to be held accountable. The public clamors for efficiency. But research cannot evaluate efficiency without measures of effectiveness. There can be no criteria of effectiveness without a cultural rationale, a community consciousness, out of which the norms build.

One of the chief fallacies of our time has been to assume that social forms control individuals. If that is true—or, to put the point another way, if it is not true that changed individuals can change institutions—then all we have to look forward to is institutional research organized around program-management systems offering increasingly sophisticated service to the assumptions of the corporate state. The values that researchers share will be those of technology; the organizations that decide their work will be bureaucratic and megatronic. Is the corporate state the basis for authority, the sanctioner and judge of life? Is institutional governance mere management?

But a new and different sensibility is emerging. It can be seen in what may be called the youth perspective. This perspec-

---

[6] Paul L. Dressel, "The Problems of Evaluation," in *The New Colleges: Toward an Appraisal* (Iowa City: American College Testing Program and Association for Higher Education, 1971), p. 2.

tive is substantive and has importance for the future of institutional research. It emphasizes that the purposes of the educational experience are, first, individual self-realization; second, meaningful social interrelationships; third, vocational-technical-professional training—but training that combines technical competence with human sensibility. The youth perspective also emphasizes institutional character, achieved through involvement in social improvement and, additionally, through institutional willingness to lead students and faculty beyond theoretical, detached consideration of social conditions to the creation and implementation of change models. The youth perspective is future-oriented.

Institutional Research of the Future

Institutional research for the future, if the new sensibility prevails, will not be known for its ability to sort out the intricacies of space allocation; it will not catalog the geographical distribution of student bodies, youths' religious affiliations, managerial options for controlling campus disruptions, fiscal efficiencies, image polls, or administrative propaganda. It will, rather, concentrate on the institution rather than the individual, or, more accurately, on what the emerging youth perspective means for curriculum, governance, facilities, finances, and institutional objectives.

But how will it do this? Because the greatest need is for a future orientation in the determination of institutional priorities and management objectives, institutional researchers will need answers, from faculty and administrators and from their own observations, to the following questions: (1) How do you justify the absence of change here? Why is it important to resist innovation or experimentation? (2) Are you aware of options—in curriculum, in finance, in philosophy, or in governance configurations? What rationale is given for selecting and following an option actually used? (3) How are institutional rewards and sanctions employed—to perpetuate the status quo or to encourage change? (4) Which programs in the institution are considered exemplary? Why? (5) Are the principles of the institution provisional, without being merely opportunistic? Do practices encourage improvisation, without being capricious? (6) Is there evidence of broad support for continuous, as opposed to periodic or sporadic, self-evaluation? If this sort of research is forthcoming, researchers will be freed to think as well as compile, define rather than defend, probe more than package.

Fortunately, an awareness of these needs and changes is beginning to prompt the creation of mechanisms for meeting them. Educational Testing Service has developed an Institutional Functioning Inventory (IFI) and, in cooperation with the Regional Laboratory for the Carolinas and Virginia, has pilot-tested an Institutional Goals Inventory (IGI). These instruments are ways of determining existing functions and priorities as well as means for identifying emerging practices and objectives. The Center for Research and Development in Higher Education, Berkeley, is designing alternative models of governance, especially those calculated to take into account the interests and influence of "new" students—youth heretofore underrepresented in colleges and universities. The Western Interstate Commission for Higher Education, in cooperation with various agencies, is trying to establish educational output measures that will accommodate qualitative as well as quantitative features and yet allow the use of computerized storage and retrieval. Technology can be captured by man rather than being his captor.

Institutional research must get involved in these areas of concern, these challenges, these concentrations of activity. In the past, IR has been too circumscribed. Promises were often global; production was usually parochial. Researchers can no longer justify such motivation; institutions can no longer tolerate such products. At a time of unparalleled confusion about where we should be, as well as widespread discontent with where we are and what we are doing, the challenge now for IR is to give less attention to gate tending and bookkeeping and more attention to goal mining to show, in the end, how data were made for men, not men for the data.

CHAPTER 4

Institutional Research

Thomas R. Mason

In its broadest sense, institutional research may be defined as the systematic appraisal and evaluation of the processes and operations of institutions of higher education. From this broad point of view, institutional research includes the whole spectrum of research in higher education, from the more "basic" research on learning processes and behavior to the applied fact-finding research of an administrative assistant helping to prepare for a legislative budget hearing. The discussion here, however, will be narrowed to the scope of institutional research that is dedicated to assisting the policy-formation and decision-making processes of college or university governance.

Role of Institutional Research in Resource Allocation

The budget-making process, the process of resource allocation, is the most visible manifestation of institutional policy making. Although not all policies are explicitly reflected in the

31

budgeting process resource allocation does reflect the shaping of institutional priorities. The role of institutional research in the resource-allocation process *ought* to be that of *evaluating* the effectiveness of the use of resources toward the fulfillment of institutional goals, objectives, and priorities.

Without meaningful criteria, derived from coherent goals and objectives, the evaluation of the effectiveness of resource allocation policies is indeed an empty exercise. Warren Bryan Martin argues in his paper that "institutions of higher education are dissatisfied with practices of the past, ambiguous about existing purposes, and devoid of perspectives appropriate for the future." This indictment is difficult to disagree with in its generality. Nevertheless, colleges and universities, while they may be suffering the kind of collective neurosis implied by Martin, are not completely adrift without purpose or direction. Choices are being made, priorities are being established, and policies are being changed continuously on the basis of valuational criteria, largely implicit, and on prevailing goals, objectives, and purposes.

The fact that these criteria are largely invisible probably reflects the pluralistic nature of institutional governance. In an academic community of critical scholars, very much involved with the larger society in the politics of gaining resources, it is extremely difficult to gain consensus from all parties to a set of explicit, concrete decision-making criteria that will result in rewards for some and deprivations for others. As a result, the criteria by which institutional priorities are set, as reflected in resource allocations, remain submerged; nevertheless, they are there, perhaps only in the form of an unspoken compromise of conflicting forces acting within and upon the institution.

What the critics of higher education are saying is that the prevailing settlement—based on tradition, convention, the protection of faculty prerogatives, and political compromise—is no longer relevant, effective, or valid, by their criteria. What the reformers are trying to do is to change the prevailing criteria, but in the process of attacking them they often seem to prefer to wish them away by saying that there are no acceptable criteria.

At the same time, those who advocate application of the

principles of business management to higher education—speaking with the new vocabulary of management science, PPBS, and systems analysis—insist that effectiveness and efficiency can be measured only if specified goals, preferably reduced to quantitative objectives, are defined.

Whichever point of view one prefers to take, goals, objectives, purposes, values, prejudices, motives, expectations, and opinions are the most significant kinds of "data" at work in the determination of fiscal policy in colleges and universities. These are the data that institutional research must probe, analyze, and order if it is to make an effective contribution to the planning and policy-making processes of institutional governance. I agree fully with Martin that "the challenge now for IR is to give less attention to gate tending and bookkeeping and more attention to goal mining."

The problem is this: A well-swung pick into the pit face of the institutional mine will uncover as many pieces of "goal" as there are individuals acting in the policy-making process. Some of these actors do not even agree with the most common identifiable goal, that of institutional survival. Of course, the vast majority will agree that our institutions should be preserved; however, consensus on the nature of their educational missions and the best means of effectively fulfilling those missions, agreement on the nature and pacing of changes in structure and processes, and, above all, general concurrence on the proper or "relevant" content of educational communication can never be fully achieved. It seems to me to be acutely naïve to expect any community of independent, strong-minded, and critically trained scholars (including those under the age of thirty) to concur on concise, explicit criteria for determining priorities and evaluating the effectiveness of institutional programs. The determination of goals and priorities, in this society, is a political process; and the basic consensus required is agreement on the processes by which conflicting values are to be resolved in a cooperative social organization.

If the goals, objectives, and priorities to be applied in the policy-formation processes of a college are determined politically, what has institutional research to do with policy-making? How can it contribute to the shaping of institutional priorities and the allocation of resources to fulfill those priorities?

Assessing Consequences and Evaluating Attitudes

I believe that in almost any type of political process the ancient urge of the human being to apply reason, logic, and the canons of scientific method to the solution of problems and to the prediction of the future remains powerful. Policy-making systems are constantly searching for ways of reducing the scope and intensity of conflict by seeking better information about an issue, by assessing the costs and consequences of alternative courses of action, and, significantly, by evaluating the values, opinions, and attitudes of the internal and external constituencies of the organization. Institutional research has emerged in response to this need for valid information and careful analysis and evaluation.

In the development of information, analyses, and predictions bearing on policy issues, the institutional-research function has a special role. If it is to be effective, institutional research must gain credibility among the participants in the process by its objectivity. However, reasonable objectivity for IR does not mean vacuous neutrality. It means explicit acknowledgment both of the assumptions upon which institutional research is based and of the limitations of the validity of its data.

I have found that the best model for organizing research in a policy-making environment is that associated with contemporary decision theory, although its basic framework dates back to antiquity. In its idealized form this research approach is as follows:

Identification and definition of the problems and issues. (Institutional research is often expected to perform a monitoring role in which it seeks to identify problems before they become crises. When a policy issue is taking shape, the delineation of the issue into a research problem may actually have the effect of crystallizing the issue—a potentially dangerous side effect.)

Collection of data bearing on the given problem or issue, including data on values, preferences, attitudes. (The timing of an issue frequently limits the amount of data collection that can be done. In many cases, acquisition of data is simply impossible. Consequently, researchers often must make assumptions about the real world on the basis of limited information; in these instances, such assumptions and limitations must be specifically spelled out.)

Analysis of the problem in light of the available data. (This is the point at which the problem is modeled, the interrelationships of the factors involved are analyzed, alternative solutions are identified, or feasible courses of action are charted.)

Evaluation of alternative solutions or courses of action. (Assessment of the costs and consequences of various alternatives and evaluation of the potential benefits, in the light of differing value criteria, usually must be based on judgments, inferences, and assumptions—which, again, should be carefully spelled out.)

I have referred to this process as the translation of data into information and the intelligent evaluation of information in the light of competing values, goals, and objectives acting in the policy-making environment. The addition of "intelligence" —the evaluation of relevant values or preferences—is, I believe, the essential step that makes an institutional research study meaningful. For the most part, this kind of evaluation is the only means we have to assess the vital "benefits" side of the cost-benefit equation. In the area of fiscal management, the least-cost criterion too often prevails when only the cost side is revealed in "hard" quantitative data. Without the evaluation of qualitative, often intangible benefits, resource-allocation policy is little more than bookkeeping.

Surfacing Submerged Goals

In the process of carrying out research and analysis in the decision-model framework, I have found that submerged institutional goals, objectives, and longer-range perspectives can be brought to the surface. That is, first a statement of *explicit* assumptions about objectives and priorities is made; then, as these assumptions are debated, accepted, acted upon, revised, or rejected, the objectives of a given policy tend to take clear shape, and in the process the criteria for setting institutional priorities on a variety of other policy issues begin to emerge.

This is not to say that institutional research can invoke a grand consensus on institutional goals and priorities. It can, through careful analysis of quantitative information and qualitative values bearing on particular policy issues, help to clarify the directions in which the institution is moving, and it can raise the questions of where the institution ought to be moving. Any institutional research study that merely looks backward and describes what was, without placing its findings in the context of the future, is incomplete and inadequate. Priorities, especially those associated with resource allocations, must be developed in terms of some array of institutional objectives. Institutional research can and must play a major role in the search for objectives.

Goals, objectives, and priorities in any human organization are driven by the motives, values, and emotions of the individuals involved in the organization. The channeling of individual values into collective goals and objectives is a political process. (Some prefer to call this process "management.") The first obligation of the institutional researcher is to understand that process thoroughly. His second obligation is to try to sustain the model of rationality in the policy-making process. While institutional research may not be able to do much to cure institutional neuroses caused by conflict, confusion, and the identity crisis, it cannot give up the struggle to sustain the uses of reason.

PART II

INTERNAL GOVERNANCE AND EXTERNAL COOPERATION

Intramural and extramural cooperation both have human, managerial, and fiscal aspects; and both raise questions of institutional autonomy. It is the existence of these common features that permits chapters on governance, on collective bargaining, and on interinstitutional cooperation to be grouped together in a single section.

Patterns of governance are changing. The questions "Who governs?" "In relation to what constituencies?" and even "In what sense does anyone govern the university?" are being asked again and fresh answers are being given. These philosophical questions about governance must receive first attention—an approach that academe finds congenial. The fiscal aspects, however, should not be overlooked in the determination of which of several forms of governance may be satisfactory. Patterns of governance must compete with other institutional priorities for fiscal attention. *Frederic W. Ness* reviews these changing patterns and, consonant with the theme of this volume, points out many of their fiscal aspects.

Collective bargaining is a special form of intramural cooperation even though it assumes an adversary relationship between faculty and administration. *Neil Bucklew* leaves for others the detailed economic analysis of specific items presented in various collective-bargaining proposals and concentrates instead on the fiscal implications of the collective-bargaining process itself: the institutional structure that must be created to maintain the process, the cost analyses that the institution must make of various proposals, and the effects of the process on institutional planning.

One form of voluntary cooperation among institutions that has been commanding an increasing amount of attention is the consortium. It has often been pursued for one reason but retained for others. The householder who is persuaded to buy a home freezer by the argument that he will be able to live more cheaply, and who later discovers that he lives not more cheaply but better, is like many a college that enters into a consortium for reasons of economy but stays because of other benefits. *Herbert H. Wood,* nevertheless, presents concrete suggestions for saving money through a consortium. An enthusiast for cooperative structures, he is eager, however, that the right thing be done for the right reasons. He pinpoints many of the costs of cooperation among institutions and identifies at the same time some ways of analyzing the financial benefits of cooperation.

CHAPTER 5

Campus Governance and Fiscal Stability

Frederic W. Ness

Campus governance has been changing so radically in recent years that no one can really predict what it is likely to be even by the end of this decade. What this means, among other things, is that the fiscal implications of governance patterns probably cannot be analyzed or precisely anticipated. One thing seems fairly clear: The traditional power elements (trustees, administrators, faculty, students), accustomed to living together in more or less amiable hostility, are finding the game rather more complex—not just because of inner tensions but because of new forces from without.

A variety of determinative factors affect governance patterns in universities today. To those identified by Eldon L. Johnson of the University of Illinois—the growth and complexity of the institution, the bureaucratization of higher education, the tactics of organized confrontation, the current antipathy to authority, the making off-campus of decisions formerly made on campus, and the crumbling of old alliances [1] —we must add the public disenchantment with higher education and the concurrent financial crunch. Thus, at a time when wise fiscal management calls for a closing of ranks, the movement seems to be centrifugal instead of centripetal.

On the surface this might not seem actually to be the case. For the dominant factor in recent developments in campus governance has been a sharing of authority. In many instances the principle of consultation has advanced from a privilege to a right, and consultation in policy matters has been converted to full partnership in decision making. Public accountability, however, has remained the exclusive and dubious privilege of the administration.

Rationalizing the right to share in governance has become etched in philosophical concrete. The problem, however, is not in the theory. It is in the implementation. When a small college in the Midwest announces that it is scheduling a regular day off in midweek to provide for and "emphasize student and faculty participation in decision-making committees," the cart seems to be getting ahead of the horse. At the very least, this kind of participation in governance will require an allocation of institutional resources drawn from more traditional production. At the other end of the scale, when a state-wide coordinating board decrees that all proposals for major academic developments in any of the tax-supported institutions or systems must be submitted to it before they can be considered by the individual boards of trustees, things seem to be even more topsy-turvy. No less a university than Yale is now proposing, with the presumed concurrence of the president, that special commissions be set up at a variety of levels for the purpose of obliging the administrators routinely to explain the reasons for their decisions to faculty, students, nonprofessional personnel, and alumni. The danger, as Eldon Johnson expresses it in another

[1] *From Riot to Reason* (Urbana: University of Illinois Press, 1971), pp. 55–57.

context, is that "In the university's circulatory system, infinite and interminable talk becomes a coagulant which produces embolism and, eventually, paralysis." [2] That interminable talk has fiscal implications is self-evident.

Any exercise of authority, of course, carries with it responsibilities and commitments, which the proponents are often wary of accepting. Faculty members often complain about the amount of time they have to spend in committee work. Yet work-load patterns incorporate committee activities as part of the normal expectations. Student participants cannot expect to be taken very seriously unless they elect effective representatives and unless these representatives are willing to do their homework. In any case, each new generation of participants must be reeducated at a substantial cost in time and energy. Administrators are not free of fault either. All too often they exert authority without at the same time exercising vigilance to assure that they deserve the right. For regardless of legalisms, effective governance must always rest upon the consent of the governed. Even the trustees, who are at the heart of many a campus problem, must be willing to take their responsibilities more seriously if we are to avert some of the less desirable patterns of governance that threaten us.

Let us look at these four components of the power structure in more detail, beginning in reverse order.

Trustees

Some critics condemn the prevailing system of collegiate trusteeship as an anachronism. A comprehensive study conducted by Morton Raugh in 1968–69 underscores such a view.[3] With their average years in the mid-fifties, with social and economic backgrounds bearing a striking and monotonous similarity, with a general sharing of undistinguished conservatism, trustees signalize dramatically the age gap between college youth and the Establishment; moreover, according to critics,

[2] *From Riot to Reason*, p. 73.
[3] *The Trusteeship of Colleges and Universities* (New York: McGraw-Hill, 1969).

they can scarcely be viewed as representative of the broad public trust inherent in the office.

That the trustee system may run into problems seems a real possibility. A questionnaire distributed at a recent meeting of the American Association for Higher Education found only 365 out of some 570 respondents favorably disposed to the present concept of the lay governing board; included among the negative were no fewer than 118 administrators.[4] In other words, dissatisfaction with the system is not found only among faculty and students. Such dissatisfaction with top management —and if the trustees are not top management, then they have little *raison d'être*—is not conducive to fiscal stability.

Part of the criticism, however, lies in the belief that the trustees are concerned too exclusively with the fiscal aspects of management, failing to see it in its broader implications. One of the most articulate attacks upon trusteeship appears in the report of the Yale University Study Commission on Governance (1971), which found that Yale trustees are drawn overwhelmingly from a narrow stratum of society and are guilty of undervaluing "the importance of scientific, educational, and research leadership in favor of financial, business, and administrative leadership."[5] The implication is that only by a more responsive reconstitution of its membership could this board merit the retention of its powers.

A political solution elected by some institutions has been to place faculty and students on their boards of trustees. As of the latest report, only 3 per cent of a national sample of colleges and universities had resorted to this expedient.[6] A weakness in this practice of representation, from a management standpoint, lies in the impact that student-faculty presence can have on the position of the president vis-à-vis his board. If he is no

---

[4] *AGB Notes,* 1971 2(5), 3. See also T. R. McConnell, *The Redistribution of Power in Higher Education: Changing Patterns of Internal Governance* (Berkeley, Calif.: Center for Research in Higher Education, 1971).

[5] *Report of the Study Commission on Governance* (New Haven: Yale University, Office of the Secretary, 1971), p. 25.

[6] R. T. Harnett, *Research Bulletin* (Princeton: Educational Testing Service, February, 1970).

longer the chief spokesman for the board to the campus and the chief representative of the campus to the board, his position of leadership cannot help being compromised. Perhaps the recognition of this danger is one reason why even the Yale Commission did not recommend such membership. Many would find student-faculty representation on boards much more acceptable, of course, if they were invited from some other academic institutions.

Presidential authority and responsibility can also be compromised under an alternative system of joint committees between board and campus. Here the temptation for faculty and students to make end runs around the administration becomes almost irresistible. This can be particularly critical in the sensitive matter of allocating institutional resources.

To improve the effectiveness of trustees and to minimize the alienation that often exists between the campus and its board, there has recently been proposed the establishment of a system of trustees-in-residence, whereby each member of the board would commit himself annually to a week of living on campus—attending classes, dining (and we presume drinking) with students and faculty, sitting in on committee meetings, the whole gamut. Let me say only that if I were the president, I would be tempted to take my bottle of Equanil and disappear into the Maine woods.

President

Under even the best of circumstances the role of the president in governance is difficult if not, as some concede, impossible. On the one hand, the president has been severely criticized for failure to exercise strong leadership in these days of campus uncertainty. On the other, a recent national survey of faculty opinion reveals that at least this element of the power grid considers the administration much too dominant in the great majority of campuses and calls for a curtailment of that power.[7] So what is the poor man to do!

[7] Reported by Morris Keeton, *Shared Authority on Campus* (Washington, D.C.: American Association for Higher Education, 1971), p. 21.

Some would urge the transplanting to these shores of a British administrative system based on the "amiable amateur." From personal observations a year or two back at a number of English universities, however, I would have to note that academic governance is undergoing changes even there—changes toward more and stronger central authority. Furthermore, despite what McConnell refers to as the "unwillingness of the academic to consider expertise in administration an academic 'specialty.' " [8] With the advent of such complex management systems as those now being developed by WICHE (Western Interstate Commission on Higher Education) it is almost incomprehensible that we will long be able to accommodate the frequently amateurish approach evident in even our present system.

Notwithstanding the chief executive's managerial and political ability (or lack thereof), the great problem of the day in academic governance is still that the president, in far too many of our institutions, is held accountable for activities over which he is denied all but the most token authority. If he survives, it is because he is phenomenally lucky or has developed administrative techniques all but unknown several decades ago. The trick, perhaps, is for him to give the appearance of sharing authority without in fact yielding it. Yet the number of Philadelphia lawyers around our campuses with time on their hands makes this next to impossible. The ideal would seem to be sharing with the faculty the formulation of policy but reserving for the president and his staff the decision-making authority. Only in this way can the power of the purse assure an adequate degree of fiscal stability. But many administrations are already far too far down the road of no return.

Students

The current thrust toward student power in governance is anything but simple. Nor is it new. Such involvement is

[8] McConnell, *Redistribution of Power*, pp. 21–22.

cognate with the founding of the first modern universities, in medieval times, when bands of students began hiring and firing their own faculties. At present, according to Earl J. McGrath, 88.3 per cent of the 875 institutions replying to a survey in 1969 admit students to membership in at least one policy-making body. Of these, 2.7 per cent grant students voting privileges on boards of trustees, and an astonishing 41 per cent admit students to committees on faculty selection, promotion, and tenure. In only twelve of these latter, however, do the students have the right to vote.[9]

Obviously it is hard to be against student participation, or even student legislative power in many areas of campus governance. There is evidence, though, that the academic administrator is more amenable to student participation than are his faculty colleagues—which suggests that he may feel its power somewhat less threatening. Also, faculty enthusiasm varies with the specific area of responsibility. In an attitude survey conducted in 1969 by Wilson and Gaff, two thirds of the sample (six diverse colleges and universities) were willing to give students responsibility for formulating social regulations; 60 per cent were even willing to offer them a voice in academic policy. When, however, the question became one of actual voting power on educational issues, the percentage dropped to 36, with only 9 per cent willing to give students an equal vote with the faculty.[10] Thus, curricular decisions that have fiscal implications are still not particularly responsive to the political thrust from the student power center.

As many observers have noted, the real struggle for power on campus is becoming more and more a contest between students and faculty. When Hunter College in 1970 sought to revamp its governance, the administration was forced to provide a professional arbitrator to help resolve the conflicts resulting from various polarizations among and between students and faculty.

A helpful approach to the general problem was proposed

[9] *Should Students Share the Power?* (Philadelphia: Temple University Press, 1970), pp. 38–50.
[10] Reported in McConnell, *Redistribution of Power*, pp. 46–47.

by Rutgers president Edward J. Bloustein, then at Bennington College, whereby each component in the power structure is provided a kind of weighted status based upon his expected degree of short- and long-term commitment to the institution. This would offer a more comprehensive involvement without necessarily tying the hands of those who must be held accountable.[11]

Before leaving this admittedly superficial overview of student participation in governance, I want to observe two possible and opposite trends. For whatever it may be worth as a bellwether, the students at the University of Chicago, after several years of ill-contained aggressiveness, have this past year evinced little or no interest in managing the university. Commenting on the inactivity of one of the most important joint committees, a spokesman said: "That committee just disintegrated; nobody is willing to take on the hard work associated with governance of the university." To curb any unduly enthusiastic reaction to this development, I must quickly add the caveat that we should not be surprised "if organized action for collective power *as students* on their campuses is a striking feature of American student life in the decades to come." [12]

What is quite impossible to ascertain is the cost of student participation. On the surface it often seems to engage an inordinate amount of administrative and faculty time; and time is money in a college as well as in any other type of industry. Also there is evidence of student pressure, in the heat of a current issue, forcing unwise decisions on the allocation of resources. On the other hand, student judgment is often quite valuable. Failure to heed it, or significantly to involve students in policy decisions, can destroy the most careful fiscal planning. Further, there is at least one instance when the students, fully understanding the college's budgetary planning, voted to request a hundred-dollar increase in tuition fees.

[11] "A New Academic Social Contract," *Liberal Education*, 1970, *56*, 10–16.

[12] Lunsford and Duster, 1970; quoted by McConnell, *Redistribution of Power*, p. 47.

Faculty

Eldon Johnson, one of the most astute and articulate critics of the governance scene, has predicted that faculty over the country will have a more influential but also more tightly structured role than heretofore—whether that role is grabbed by power, conceded as good administration, or negotiated calmly. Still, it might not be too much to say that what we see generally throughout the academic profession verges on the anachronistic.

As represented by the organization and premises of the American Association of University Professors, academic governance has been postulated on the vestigial remnants of the earlier scholar-guild tradition, a tradition that exists practically nowhere else with equal definition among those who are not self-employed. The evidence is strong, moreover, that this is a waning force. Donald Wolleth, labor law professor at the University of California at Davis, declares flatly that collective bargaining will become "the primary vehicle for faculty participation" in collegiate governance.[13] Even the AAUP has now come down on the side of collective bargaining. The question is why this new movement is gaining such momentum; and the answers are far from simple. One reason, certainly, is that administrators and even trustees are increasingly insisting upon greater faculty accountability. This inevitably threatens the autonomy of the faculty and sets up tensions that encourage collective measures for self-protection. Second, the fiscal bind on most campuses is curtailing both the steady advances of salaries and the parallel decline in productivity. Since the controlling decisions in such matters, for perhaps 70 per cent of the nation's college faculties, are being made by agencies that exist beyond the purlieus of the campus, collective resistance appears to many to be the only recourse. Concurrently, legislatures and even boards of trustees are calling into question such sacred prerogatives as tenure and teaching loads, and these are readily (though erroneously) interpreted by a defensive faculty

[13] *Business Week*, May 1, 1971, p. 69.

as attacks upon that most sacred of principles, academic freedom.

Third, though rarely admitted, the very growth of student power on an organized, nationwide basis may be conducive to a collective response from the professoriat. It is true, of course, that some "faculty unions have courted student alliances in times of extreme crisis—when the object of attack is the same but for different reasons; but in platforms and prospectuses, they are volubly silent on siding with the students." [14] This difference may become all the more pronounced as student sophistication increases and as students come to recognize the resistance of faculty power to the attainment of some of their cherished objectives. The National Students Association is, in fact, considering measures that will make it a third party in all collective-bargaining confrontations.

Fourth, within the faculty itself the rapid expansion of recent years has exacerbated the natural tension between the younger and the older professors. Under the guild system the power lies in the hands of the tenured—that is, the older —faculty. Under the union's one-man-one-vote system, the younger faculty stand a much better chance of evading the "tyranny of the old guard."

Finally, this expansion of the faculty has opened the profession to many new and varying traditions. In the old days many went into college teaching as a means of upward mobility, escaping the worker's status, much as was true with the medical profession. This is far less prevalent today, possibly because college teaching has lost some of its luster. A study by Ann M. Heiss of Berkeley shows that well over 50 per cent of doctoral candidates in the nation's ten leading graduate schools would join a teaching assistant's union if one existed on their campus.[15] It is hardly likely that these same individuals would eschew unionism once they became regular members of a faculty.

What is clear is that we are rapidly moving into a period

[14] Johnson, *From Riot to Reason*, p. 70.
[15] *Challenges to Graduate School* (San Francisco: Jossey-Bass, 1970).

of immense complexity in faculty governance. Some campuses are already experiencing the problems of rival and competing unions, with one representing the regular faculty, another representing the student-assistant and part-time staff. The Association of American Law Schools, in behalf of the law faculty at Fordham University, filed an amicus brief urging the NLRB to adopt "a policy of preferring to place law faculty in a bargaining unit separate from other university faculty" on the grounds that the law faculty's "sense of identity and community of interests are separate and apart from that of the rest of the faculty." [16] Under this reasoning, so would be the faculties of medicine, dentistry, agriculture, enology, you name it. When we add to these complications the nonprofessional staff's unions, many of which are courting faculty support if not actual membership, we are confronting labor issues much more involute than those typical of American industry as a whole. Moreover, the decision is often no longer the exclusive jurisdiction of the campus itself, as state after state begins to mandate collective bargaining for college staffs in the tax-supported sectors. The administrative costs involved in reaching so many separate settlements will be incalculable.

Many independent colleges and universities still feel that they are exempt from such vexing problems. However, the recent NLRB ruling regarding Long Island University, a private institution, is much more than a mere straw in the wind. Under this complex ruling, the faculty member may participate in management when the faculty makes group decisions, but when he acts as an individual he is nonmanagement. Departmental chairmen are to be considered management, despite the fact that they are generally chosen from the faculty and by the faculty voting as individuals. Moreover, they traditionally regard themselves as faculty members. Further, by grouping full- and part-time faculty together, this awkward ruling actually runs counter to a long-standing philosophy of the AAUP that clearly separates the two.

There is every evidence that unionism will have serious

---

[16] See *Higher Education and National Affairs*, June 4, 1971, p. 8.

consequences to the profession as well as serious fiscal implications for the institution. It could well mean that the individual professor, long accepted as "a man who thinks otherwise," will lose much of his freedom of action. Faculty senates, whose powers have been so laboriously accrued over the decades, will become relatively impotent. And, as ominously predicted by McConnell (1971), a system of governance responsive to all components of the campus may never thereafter be devised. The administration, which has generally been willing to share its responsibilities with the faculty in recent years, will find itself precluded from the tradition of colleagueship, and an adversary relationship will almost inevitably replace collegiality. In the larger systems the local campuses will lose virtually all of their autonomy, since key decisions will almost certainly be negotiated at the level of the highest central authority.

One other point seems relevant here. In the industrial model, which many are seeking to transplant on the campus, management and labor are in effect negotiating for their share of the profits. When the negotiations, as they inevitably do, call for more profits, these are achieved by cutting the quality of the product, increasing productivity through technology, or advancing the cost to the consumer. Moreover, the consumers are generally scattered and disorganized. Thus we have two-party negotiations operating in relative isolation. But the consumer in college collective bargaining—the student—is present on the scene and is himself well organized or capable of being organized. It seems hardly likely that the student will stand idly by and accept either a substantial increase in the already heavy burden of charges or a decrease in the quality of educational services available to him.

In the meantime, the movement toward collective bargaining has added yet more strains upon an admittedly confused structure. Recent studies show that college and university faculties are already seriously divided—not that most of us need a study to tell us this. If, as many contend, the real power in governance will continue to reside with the faculty, then it seems almost unavoidable that our campuses run the danger of becoming deadlocked at just exactly the wrong moment of history.

At the moment we know far too little about the changing patterns of governance on either the formal or the informal level. What is clear, however, is that governance patterns have serious implications for the fiscal health of an institution. The power groups tend to be more interested in accruing authority than in being willing to accept responsibility or to be held accountable for the fiscal health of the institution. Trustees and presidents may well be accused of being reactionary when they resist inroads on their authority. The question remains, however, whether our institutions can survive through a period of financial crisis without a strong and responsible central management. The odds would seem to be all in the other direction.

CHAPTER 6

Fiscal Implications of Collective Bargaining

Neil S. Bucklew

Collective bargaining, like many other decision-making processes of our society, is a mixture of both fiscal and nonfiscal judgments and pressures. Negotiation between two parties in an attempt to reach an agreement over employment-related issues is a dynamic process. It can best be understood and explained by observations from the perspective of many disciplines. Here however we will deal only with the fiscal implications of collective bargaining.

For some, the term *collective bargaining* raises the image of horse trading. For others, it is an image of pressure politics and the unlimited use of power and persuasion. For still others the term raises the picture of two groups, each with its own calculator, determining a satisfactory way of dividing up a given amount of money. The process is obviously something more than any of these generalizations. It involves fiscal judgments made in a political context.

Cost of Infrastructure

What are the *structural requirements* of an institution of higher education as it organizes itself for the collective-bargaining decision-making process? Perhaps the term *infrastructure* is a descriptive and accurate way to refer to this aspect of fiscal analysis. The development and maintenance of such an infrastructure requires three basic elements: (1) direct personnel costs; (2) indirect personnel costs of collective bargaining; (3) costs of maintaining information systems for collective bargaining.

Direct personnel costs are the costs of maintaining an administrative office to represent the university in negotiations and the various "support" arrangements involved. If a university is to be formally involved in collective negotiations, it must have an individual administrator with this designated responsibility—sometimes the personnel officer of the university; sometimes, at larger institutions, a director of employment relations. Although the administrator involved may be a spokesman for the university and even maintain the centralized administrative responsibility for contracts negotiated, a wide range of professional support persons also are needed for these processes. The administrator, therefore, serves basically as a coordinator of collective-bargaining activities in the university.

Any analysis of these direct personnel costs must take into consideration the significant portion of time spent in collective-bargaining activities by individuals in the fiscal area of the university—the budget director, the business manager, the controller. In addition, the services of an attorney—either the university counsel or an outside attorney specializing in labor law—are frequently required. Another professional involvement (outlined in more detail below) is that of the informational services staff of the university—most notably, the director of data processing or the director of institutional research or both. Finally, as with any administrative function, clerical and technical help is needed. The "paperage" inherent in the development of a consensus position for collective bargaining is legendary among those who work in this field.

Indirect personnel costs can have a significant fiscal impact. Because the results of much collective-bargaining activity are crucial, top policy-making individuals in the organization must become involved. Parameters for bargaining are not made at the negotiating table but must be worked out at the policy level of an institution of higher education. This type of policy determination and consideration can represent a very sizable indirect personnel cost to an organization. The bargaining team must understand the basic policy and parameter considerations, as well as the full implications of collective-bargaining agreements. Such an understanding requires significant involvement in time of the supervisory personnel of the organization. Since in many ways the supervisors became the actors under the resulting collective-bargaining agreements, the agreements must provide them with a workable blueprint for many personnel-related decisions.

Another basic element in the organization's infrastructure for collective bargaining involves the maintenance of informational systems. An informational "library" is necessary not only for negotiations but for administration of the subsequent agreement. Preparation of arbitration cases, for example, requires many costly documents as reference materials. The informational system provides both external data and internal data. External data—data on other institutions and organizations that serve as a reference base for this specific institution of higher education—are developed and maintained through surveys, various reporting services, and conferences. Internal data—knowledge by the institution of its present state and its anticipated growth patterns in the personnel area—are essential to cost-analysis projects that will be used to inform the decision-making process for the university in collective bargaining.

A new question facing institutions of higher education is whether the existing structures used for staff-employee bargaining can be effective in what appears to be a new era of faculty and professional staff bargaining. A few institutions—apparently seeking a more subtle and "reasoned" relationship than that perceived to exist in staff negotiations—are developing new structures or are using only certain parts of their existing staff-employee collective-bargaining structure. Such a response may in fact be a critical commentary on staff negotiations in institutions of higher education.

Costing of Proposals

For the administration of an institution of higher education, a cost analysis of negotiation proposals and agreements requires two basic costing exercises. The first is to gain a clear understanding of potential resources for the issues being considered in collective bargaining. The university needs a grasp of the resources available to be applied toward the issues in question. It is difficult, if not impossible, for the negotiating team to represent the university professionally if it does not have a clear understanding of the fiscal parameters in which the university operates. The employee representatives involved are equally concerned with having some understanding of the scope of the resources.

The other basic exercise involved in this costing area is the ability to understand the fiscal implications of proposals made by employee representatives. One of the hidden difficulties is the error of omission when the inherent cost of a proposal or agreement is not fully understood.

Many proposals made can be costed on a direct basis. A salary demand or proposal—whether it is a percentage system, a step program, a merit system, or some combination—can be costed with some degree of accuracy. Most fringe-benefit programs also fall into the area of direct costing. Most institutions with collective-bargaining experience have direct-costing considerations as a crucial part of their decision-making, although this is not always true for specific proposals. Indirect costing, however, is frequently overlooked—at a very real cost to the university—although indirect costs could be anticipated by adequate planning. For instance, a proposal that requires administrative programs and monitoring during the life of the contract has significant subsequent costs in administrative and support staff time. Another indirect cost is that of the development of joint programs or committees. Committee time and cost cannot realistically be taken lightly or viewed simply as an "easy, cheap way out." Another area of indirect costs is the demonstration effect of a particular agreement; that is, the extension of a particular benefit to one employee group has a significant effect on the desires and demands of other employee groups in the university community. The resulting costs of what may appear to be an insignificant item in one negotiation can be heavily felt in subsequent negotiations with other employee groups.

Another important issue to consider in the costing of proposals and agreements is that of the long-term cost of a proposal. A first response is to consider the short-term value or cost (during the life of the contract). Most agreements, however, continue in effect beyond the life of the particular agreement or contract and have a pyramiding, or growing, effect. It might be noted parenthetically that the long-term effect of a particular proposal needs to be viewed in the light of the best estimate of the future operations of the institution. What may appear to be a reasonable and rational proposal for overtime can have a very different effect five years hence, when the growth of the institution has outstripped the personnel resources of a particular market.

Costing models can be valuable aids in the costing of proposals and agreements. These models are computer-based methods of making both simple and complex evaluations of proposals. For example, a university can use such a model to obtain an adequate evaluation of the potential pay systems that may be proposed by employee organizations. Employee-profile information (rank, degrees, work-load averages, and other information that could conceivably be used as a basis for a salary proposal on the part of the employee group) can be built into a formula or set of formulas for various levels of percentage increases or other potential employee pay-scale proposals. The models can be preplanned and can produce very accurate cost data as a way of evaluating particular proposals.

Effect on Institutional Planning

A final consideration in fiscal implications of collective bargaining is its effect on the broader issue of fiscal planning for the institution. Collective bargaining is simply an optional way to deal with certain personnel issues. In effect, it is a decision-making process for the organization. If the decisions that eventually result from bargaining are to be workable, both parties involved must have a common base of information regarding the fiscal life of the university. This implies a posture of full disclosure of information relating both to the development of the budget and to the subsequent allocation of funds for the institution. Until the employee organizations recognize the general fiscal structure and situation of the organization, there is little potential for a continuing attitude of fiscal responsibility on their part. Full disclosure and discussion do not, obviously, guarantee such an attitude, but they do represent the minimal framework if such an attitude is to be encouraged and maintained.

One goal of the university in negotiations should be to develop on the part of its employee representatives a full understanding of the fiscal limitations and possibilities of the university and the priority judgments at work on the part of the institution. Even if the employee representatives maintain what could be described as unrealistic demands in the face of this information, it is improbable that withholding the information would have produced any different response. There is ample evidence that such a relationship of full information can produce a more responsible and understanding attitude on the part of employee organizations.

It is not enough simply to share budget planning and subsequent allocation information with employee organizations. Since public and private institutions differ from one another in the complexities of their financing and in the constraints under which they must operate in pursuing funds for their programs, each university should undertake a positive program of exposing employee groups to the complexities and realities of the financing of higher education in our society. The complexities differ between public institutions and private institutions. Each has a unique framework in which it must pursue the financing of its programs. Employee groups may put forth "extreme" proposals not because of a basically destructive or unconcerned attitude but because of an inadequate understanding of the resources available or the processes involved.

There will be some impulse on the part of employee groups to deal with the "source" of financing for institutions of higher education. In the public sector they will wish to deal as directly as possible with the legislative or executive group involved in the basic financial decisions for institutions of higher education. In the private sector they will wish to deal with the board or the parent body of the institution. This is seldom conducive to effective and meaningful negotiations on an ongoing basis, but the impulse is not an unnatural one on the part of groups in a bureaucratic environment.

The fiscal implications of collective bargaining are most fully recognized when they are viewed and experienced as more than a necessary but limited tool. They offer a structure for informed decision-making as well.

CHAPTER 7

Financial Aspects of Cooperation among Institutions

Herbert H. Wood

Cooperative activities among colleges and universities during the past decade have shown a marked growth and now give every indication of becoming an important characteristic of higher education. For many institutions of higher education the question is no longer whether they should participate in cooperative relationships with other colleges and universities. Rather, the question is how to select the most promising programs or projects; how to determine the costs of cooperation and the ways in which cooperative efforts can be most effective.

Growth of Consortia

Where voluntary cooperative arrangements have been formalized, such groupings of institutions are called "consortia." Voluntary cooperation is the feature that distinguishes these associations from state-wide systems of coordination imposed by legislative statute. By present count, over 693 private and public colleges and universities, from the largest to the smallest, have formally associated themselves in 70 consortia, each substantial enough to have a full-time administrator, two or more academic programs requiring long-term financial commitment, and three or more institutions participating. What is significant is that eighteen of these major consortia were organized after 1970; only nine were in existence prior to 1961. These consortia serve institutions in forty-seven states, in several Canadian provinces, and even in Great Britain.

State of the Art

While cooperation among colleges and universities has been going on for some time, a close and systematic relationship with evidence of enduring ties is a development still in its infancy. The state of the art of interinstitutional cooperation is primitive, and consortia are well short of realizing their potential in almost every case. There are a few principles emerging that seem to apply generally to the process of cooperation. However, much is still in the experimental stage.

For example, it is not known whether a promising project for one group of colleges will turn out to be as advantageous for another group. Such variables as campus leadership, quality of coordination, particular needs of member institutions, the geographical spread of membership, and the history of success and failures of the cooperating group concerned will determine which of several potential projects is most promising.

There are few pilot models to demonstrate how effective cooperation can be. One has only to scan progress reports of projects under way among institutions of higher education to realize how modest present achievements are as compared with the potential service any one of the successful projects could provide to participating institutions. It is important, therefore, that the lively experimentation going on in various parts of the nation be adequately reported. Exploration of the next cooperative steps, avoidance of effort that leads to dead-end programs, and adequate description of projects that have matured are essential to a developing consortium.

It is important in analyzing a consortium to recognize that, as a result of the kinds of tasks it is generally asked to perform, it is not an institution in its own right. It operates as a kind of supporting agency whose effectiveness is measured by its impact on the operations of each of its member institutions. Consequently, the consortium should be preoccupied with its consultation and implementing processes rather than with its organizational structure. This is not widely understood; and too often time is diverted to matters of charters, bylaws, and formal jurisdictional questions. Such structural matters are benchmarks of progress. The reality of interinstitutional cooperation is found, however, in the dynamics of working relationships between individuals and the kinds of support that sustain them— such as mutual confidence, manpower for following up decisions, and mutual stimulation for creative new approaches to problems.

There are many kinds of consortia. Some are composed of institutions of a certain type; some have undertaken to acquire membership of large as well as small institutions; some include all institutions of higher education in a given area or region; some see their relationship as preliminary to eventual merger while others found in opposition to this goal their first point of agreement. An even greater measure of distinctiveness among consortia may be seen in the level of activity, the degree of campus involvement, the enthusiasm of their membership for reform and change, and the member institutions' acceptance of interinstitutional ties and obligations. The consortia movement, if such it is, may soon be classified on the basis of activity patterns rather than institutional composition.

Mounting costs of operation have been a chief stimulant for institutions to join cooperative activities. The more effective utilization of staff and resources is an important element in consortia goals. It turns out, however, that cutting operational expenses is neither sought nor achieved as a primary objective once a consortium is under way. In practice, most consortia view providing services to participating institutions and their students—services that could not be provided as effectively or economically by each institution on its own—as their primary objective.

Too often, institutions set about establishing consortia with unrealistic expectations. Some optimistically believe that if activities are pooled, the increased volume will reduce costs and there will be little or no expense for the required coordination. However, coordination has two kinds of expenses: those associated with the central coordination that puts the individual campus parts together into a single functioning operation, and those on the participating campuses that interface with the coordinated effort. The campus costs involve meetings among participating institutions to set policies as well as for on-campus functions and routine processing activities. Accurate identification of these expenses will eliminate from further consideration some otherwise attractive programs.

Anticipating the financial requirements for cooperation is difficult; yet some estimate of the cost of its level of activity must be made each year, and appropriate campus budget allowances must be set aside in anticipation of the year's requirements. There are dangers here. If a fixed ceiling of programs or level of activities is established in advance, with the implication that unexpected or emerging opportunities during the year will be refused, the consortium will likely develop a measure of sterility and will have destroyed one of its greatest assets—a dynamism to motivate new approaches and new solutions. The discovery of institutional needs is not an annual event. A consortium, however, is not an educational institution and should not be expected to function like one when the coming year's budget is being planned.

The task of the consortium's management is to anticipate the basic core of staff and activities needed. This includes what could be called "program-generation machinery." Since building next year's plans and proposals often involves the same coordinators that administer this year's programs, program generation and program supervision fall within the same core package.

Beyond the core budget, a special-projects category can be used to reflect the ups and downs of annual funding, shifts in program emphasis, or new directions. Moving away from a hand-to-mouth annual "go-no-go" on the entire cooperative effort is essential to the maturation of a consortium. The consortium that fails to achieve at least a minimal core maintenance level will probably not survive, and the early years of effort invested in developing that consortium will be lost.

Cost-Benefit Analysis

If an effective consortium is one that helps its member institutions do a better job in providing educational services to students, the most significant benefits of a consortium should be those found in ongoing campus activities. A cost-benefit analysis of consortium services needs to include these indirect relationships, and they are not easily identified. Several factors inhibit such identification.

A consortium cannot provide a full panorama of services —only those that each individual institution could not provide as adequately for itself. Some services do not have a suitable or advantageous collective-action approach. Often, the limitedness of consortium services is not understood by participating institutions anxious to receive services directly related to specific problems threatening their survival. Some institutions have even faulted a consortium for failing to provide specific benefits which, according to charter and purpose, the consortium is not allowed to provide.

A consortium also has limited impact on the current

operating budgets of participating institutions. Except in the case of unrestricted funds, cooperative program funds can replace only a minor portion of an institution's budget. Some unrestricted funds can be obtained through a joint application, under the aegis of a consortium, to carry out activities solely on individual member-college campuses. Foundations and other agencies have seen fit to identify and fund groups of colleges and universities in this way. The recipient institutions, on their part, have not been reluctant to accept such funding, even though cooperative aspects are largely missing. Such joint funding for individual purposes should not be overlooked. With care and proper institutional expectations, a consortium can venture into this area when opportunity presents itself. Acquiring funds for member institutions should be considered as a benefit, particularly if its conditions and consequences are understood. Flexibility in consortium operations should be maintained for the sake of such benefits of membership.

However, there is danger in member institutions' continuing to expect this type of special benefit from a consortium. Such funding does little to encourage significant and enduring cooperative effort, and may pose a special threat to the consortium's survival should the funding be terminated. In the long run, a consortium will find greater success in obtaining funds for cooperative efforts than for those that are not cooperative.

Further limiting the financial impact of consortium operations on the budget of member institutions is the fact that the modest grants for cooperative efforts must be divided among participating institutions. A $40,000 project in a consortium budget may appear to be a substantial program; when it is extended to twenty member institutions, however, the cost-benefit analysis per institution should be based upon $2,000. Consortia have prospered in part because member institutions have accepted this division and have carefully selected projects that have produced benefits on each campus which, in some instances, approach the entire project size. From the donor's point of view, there is a big return on the dollar.

When the portion of a participating institution's budget

open to cooperative program impact is considered, and institutional support under the aegis of the consortium has run its course, the possibility of a consortium's providing greater support than between 3 and 5 per cent of institutional budgets seems remote. In terms of direct funds, in other words, a consortium cannot assure a member institution's survival.

Most difficult of all is measurement of those indirect benefits to a member institution—benefits that provide, over the years, the subtle changes that make the institution attractive to students and to able staff and instructors. Faculty development activities, new and different learning opportunities for students, additional library resources, in-service training experience of administrative staff, access to jointly owned resources such as computers, and the continual exchange of ideas among staff, instructors, and students of the various member institutions will have significant impact.

If, because of a consortium's projects, a given campus takes on a certain sparkle and attractiveness, would it be possible openly to attribute this to the consortium rather than to that institution's own leaders? What value can one place on bringing a member institution a bit closer to the mainstream of higher education? What specific project costs should be used in providing the analysis of such a benefit? Instead of careful cost-benefit evaluation, what generally happens is that for diverse reasons a pleased membership simply decides to keep the consortium going for another year.

Consortium benefits tend, therefore, to be measured not in specific benefits against the cost of specific projects but rather in their cumulative effect upon the well-being and attractiveness of the participating institutions. Individual projects, it is true, are considered for continuance on the basis of whether anything came of them. The usual criteria are the level of activity, the corresponding interest of participating campus staff, the project's multiplier effect in the form of new projects or modifications, and—often the final determinant of priorities —the availability of funds beyond institutional resources.

What has been said above does not take into account the special circumstances of merger. Some benefits of joint operation are beyond the reach of a consortium structure. If maintenance of autonomy is not assumed, the campuses involved can be treated as branches of a single institution and a more significant measure of cost savings can be realized. Reluctance to dispense with continuing autonomy, however, should not be passed over lightly. If a goal of a consortium is to provide a diversity of educational opportunities to the general constituencies being served by members of the consortium, then maintenance of a measure of autonomy is essential.

Potential Savings

The geographical spread of a consortium's membership, as well as the interests and inclinations of faculty and staff of member institutions, will have much to do with the projects undertaken and the savings achieved. The experience of consortia suggests that savings are possible in some of the following areas:

Business-travel insurance, provided to all institutional employees, can be jointly purchased at savings up to 25 per cent over identical plans individually purchased. Personal accident insurance handled through payroll deductions and purchased through a consortium can provide savings of 5 per cent as compared with other group plans.

Medical-expense coverage, life insurance, and disability insurance, with a measure of institutional choice allowed, can be jointly purchased at a saving. Retirement plans provided through a consortium, however, appear to offer little advantage over several national programs presently available.

The purchase of training courses for supervising personnel, rather than payment of tuition for existing courses, offers advantages. The collection service of National Defense Student Loans was one of the earliest joint processing programs. Cooperative purchasing appears to have only a limited advantage within a consortium over that of several existing national and regional services. Only where guaranteed minima, central warehousing, and common agreement on specifications can be established is there a possibility of significant savings.

In the academic area, the January inter-term offers consortia a new opportunity to gather sufficient student enrollments to make many advantageous learning experiences economically feasible. While student exchanges for semester or term enrollments have long been available, only in a limited number of consortia and subject fields has significant activity been noted. Geographical proximity is a factor here, particularly when students avail themselves of courses at several institutions in the same semester. The reluctance of students to travel or to disrupt a comfortable campus-based pattern is an obstacle to greater savings.

Purchases of utility services—for instance, a telephone conferencing system, computer time sharing, and computer-related services such as programming and systems development—have proved advantageous.

Joint efforts in student recruitment and public relations seem to offer some potential. Microfilm banks and other means of sharing library periodical resources can show significant savings.

With growing emphasis on field experience as a part of a college instructional program, off-campus centers and instructional supervision can be obtained more economically through collective arrangements.

Activities Promising Greatest Effectiveness

The identification in a consortium of a given activity as one that holds promise will depend on the level of campus interest in that activity, the degree of involvement of faculty and staff, the adequacy of follow-through effort on the part of the central secretariat, the prevailing level of trust and confidence among member institutions, and the "track record" of successful efforts in the past. In selecting projects, those involved in decision making—whether weighing alternative projects or setting priorities among needed programs—should keep in mind the following considerations:

Consideration should be given to the consortium's present state of development. A complicated program, without some previous project successes, should be given a lower priority than more easily executed programs.

The level of interest on the participating campuses should be considered. Campus personnel who have given time and effort to the shaping of a new program have much to do with establishing a suitable level of campus readiness for it.

Adequate staff time should be made available to look after the program's operation and, particularly, to do the timely prodding and reminding that an interinstitutional program often needs. Insufficient central-office coordination or inadequate released time of a campus-based coordinator has weakened the effectiveness of otherwise useful programs.

Wise choices among equally desirable programs would be those with greater potential for being multipliers of additional activities or projects. One good project can often generate by-product activities, whether on participating campuses or in the cooperative effort. Some of these might even exceed the original program in ultimate value. Discussion and speculation at the time a new project is being considered can often provide clues to its potential productiveness.

Concern should be given to both the short-run and the long-run payoff potential of projects. Current programs in operation should include a balance of those of each kind. A newer consortium, however, should carry a few more with short-run payoff to pick up momentum and interest.

All contemplated programs should be examined for their direct or indirect impact on or enhancement of the learning experience of students.

Finally, the effectiveness of a college or university in meeting its goals or objectives depends upon the effectiveness of the people concerned. Cooperative programs to be desired are those that enable the faculty and staff of participating institutions to realize their potential more fully.

PART III

COSTS OF STUDENTS

There are those—and they include more than the young—who think that students are what higher education is all about. Certainly students are what the finance of higher education is all about. They must be found (admissions); subsidized (student aid); cared for (student services); and taught (instruction).

The new democracy is old hat in higher education. The idealized student-teacher ratio—one man, one prof—antedates one man, one vote by a good many years. Decidedly a labor-intensive industry, higher education has been committed to the notion that the yeasty process of human learning can be induced only by the ferment provided by intimate contact between the learner and the learned. *Rexford G. Moon, Jr., Howard R. Bowen,* and *Gordon K. Douglass* challenge the assumption that this is necessarily true for all higher learning and present both arguments and proposals for alternative ways of conducting the instructional process.

Colleges have built their student services after the fashion of the New England farmhouse. As new needs were discovered, new services were added. The result has been a rambling construction, attractive and serviceable enough after its fashion but not a very economical model and hardly a structure one would set out to build. As long as it is simpler and cheaper to add on, the process continues. But the day arrives when the whole structure is badly in need of repair, when the difficulty and expense of heating becomes acute, and when questions must be asked about refurbishing or tearing down and rebuilding to suit contemporary needs of service and of economy. That day has arrived for the rambling nature of higher education's student services. *G. Wayne Glick* raises and examines some of the questions involved.

CHAPTER 8

Beating the High Cost of Low Ratios

Rexford G. Moon, Jr.

In the race for fiscal survival, costs have been gaining every year on income. In 1969–70 costs forged ahead of income in a great many places. Things have to change. For most institutions, projecting ten years of past practices five years into the future will be a great way to go out of business. What a university of 5,500 full-time students can do today for twelve million dollars could cost almost nineteen million dollars to do in 1975–76.

What options are open? A few years back, increasing income was the panacea: spend asset appreciation; increase risk investment; get federal funds; get contract research; run big fund drives; get state funds; add more students; raise tuition. The ability to increase income almost at will in the 1960s offered absolutely no incentive to colleges to control expenses. A look into the future indicates that the private institutions—

and many public ones as well—are more likely to "find happiness" by slowing down costs enough so that income, which is getting exhausted, can struggle once again into the lead. *Serious planning for the 1970s should not be based on hopes for another income boom like the 1960s.*

If optimal use of resources, a matter of relatively little concern in the 1960s, is to be the battle cry of the 1970s, where do we start? The thesis of this paper is that *we must start with faculty productivity* and consider it the area of highest priority in achieving optimal use of resources in the decade ahead.

Although the ancient Talmud sanctified the 25 to 1 ratio of students to teacher currently popular in our public elementary and secondary schools, only recently, at least in terms of recorded history, was higher education's currently prized ratio of teacher to student established. For the benefit of those who are worried about federal control, this was done by a president of the United States—James A. Garfield. The heritage he passed on from the nineteenth century was that the ideal college would have a teacher-student ratio of 1 to 1: "Mark Hopkins on one end of a log and a student on the other."

One thing that history never told us is whether Hopkins would meet with his student all day long, five or six days a week (thereby creating as many as forty to fifty student contact hours), or at infrequent and unscheduled "class" meetings.

Faculty work load is tough to measure and study. It is a differing matter from college to college and from department to department within colleges. A recent study by the Academy for Educational Development of total student credit hours taught per faculty member in four very similar small liberal-arts colleges revealed a range from a low of 123 credit hours per faculty member in physics to a high of 613 credit hours in history. The institutions also varied considerably by subject fields. For example, a college with the lowest average load in biology proved to have the highest load in French. (See Table 1.)

We know from experience and research that work loads vary tremendously within colleges because of tradition, negotia-

TABLE 1

COMPARISON OF STUDENT CREDIT HOURS GENERATED
BY DEPARTMENT PER F.T.E. FACULTY MEMBER
AT FOUR COLLEGES, ALL LEVELS

Biology		English	
College A	124.6	College A	266.1
College B	146	College C	312
College C	224	College B	382
College D	272	College D	457

French		History	
College B	146	College B	214
College C	182	College A	318
College D	298	College C	324
College A	301	College D	613

Mathematics		Physics	
College C	168	College A	123.2
College B	182	College C	192
College A	312.7	College B	220
College D	361	College D	227

tions, and differing curricular needs. Even across institutions
of very similar type, resources, and purpose, faculty loads vary
tremendously. Some institutions have developed or are developing elaborate systems to attempt more nearly to equalize faculty
productivity—but not by adding to hours taught. In most institutions, in fact, the majority of faculty actually teach fewer
hours than the stated procedures prescribe.

In 1959, Ruml and Morrison wrote in their *Memo to
a College Trustee,* "The idea that the lower the overall ratio
of students to teachers the better the quality of instruction is
sheer fantasy." They shocked the higher education world when
they proposed that a ratio of 20 to 1, with a teaching load of
nine hours plus reasonable use of lectures and large seminars,
be resorted to in order to improve faculty compensation and
so make teaching attractive in the smaller colleges. In my
judgment, their proposal—offered as an arrangement to improve compensation and competition—will be an absolute
economic necessity in the next ten years for most colleges.

Let us look at a real college of 1,500 students that in 1960 had an average faculty total compensation of $7,500. The student-teacher ratio was 9 to 1, with 166 faculty members. The aggregate compensation of faculty in 1960 was approximately $1,245,000, or roughly $830 per enrolled student. By 1970 this same college had an average total compensation of $14,365. It was spending about $2,400,000 in aggregate compensation for faculty, or $1,600 per enrolled student. By 1980, this college says, it would like to pay average total compensation of $28,400. This will cost the college roughly $4,700,000— or $3,133 per enrolled student. (See Table 2.)

TABLE 2

RELATIONSHIP OF TUITION, FACULTY SIZE, AND
COMPENSATION IN ONE PARTICULAR COLLEGE

| | Actual | | | Options | |
	1960	1970	1980(A)	1980(B)	1980(C)
Student enrollment	1,500	1,500	1,500	1,500	1,500
Faculty numbers	166	166	166	166	93
Faculty-student ratio	1/9	1/9	1/9	1/9	1/16
Average compensation	$7,500	$14,365	$28,400	$28,400	$28,400
Tuition charge	$1,400	$2,000	$3,953	$5,327	$3,000
Aggregate compensation	$1,245,000	$2,384,590	$4,714,400	$4,714,400	$2,655,000
Tuition income	$2,100,000	$3,000,000	$5,930,000	$7,990,500	$4,500,000
Compensation as percentage of tuition income	59%	79.5%	79.5%	59%	59%

The erosion of income is obvious. In 1960 student tuition was $1,400, so that only 59 per cent of tuition income was required to pay faculty compensation. By 1970 tuition was $2,000 but now 79 per cent was required to pay faculty compensation. By 1980, if this college were to recover through tuition 59 per cent of total faculty compensation as in 1960, tuition would have to be almost $5,400. Even if 79 per cent were to be taken from tuition income in 1980 for compensation, leaving only 21 per cent of tuition income for all other purposes, tuition would have to be almost $4,000 per year.

A series of decisions by this institution to continue a student-faculty ratio of 9 to 1 and to double faculty compensation will require it to have a per-student tuition charge of between $4,000 and $5,400 per year by 1980.

If we are right about the decade of the seventies with respect to the uncertainty of income increases, it is very important that this college build more freedom into its tuition-income picture than it had in 1970.

Suppose that this college made the following decisions: (1) An upper limit of $3,000 tuition would be reached in the decade. (2) About 40 per cent of tuition income would be needed to support items other than faculty compensation. (3) It could not increase enrollment but wanted to hold with the 1,500 it had during the 1960s. (4) It wished to continue to increase total faculty compensation with a goal of doubling by 1980. How would all these decisions affect educational arrangements? In brief, under these conditions this college, by 1980, will have a faculty-student ratio of about 16 to 1 instead of the 9 to 1 that it supported during the 1960s.

What does this do to the teaching load? During the 1960s the average full-time student at our college spent about fifteen hours in the classroom each week to get the average of fifteen hours of credit. This means that during any one week the college had about 22,500 hours of instruction. On the average, each of our 166 faculty members was responsible for 135 student credit hours of instruction per week. On a nine-hour teaching load this would be about fifteen students per class.

During the seventies we are assuming that the already clear trend of about twelve hours in class by students will develop broadly. This will generate fewer actual contact hours, though the credit hours may remain the same. We may expect, in other words, that the actual hours of formal instruction in the 1970s will go down—in our college to as low as 18,000 hours per week. With this reduction in contact hours and with the planned reduction in full-time-equivalent faculty, what happens to teaching load? By 1980, ninety-three faculty covering 18,000 contact hours of instruction will have a student-contact-hour load of 193 hours per week. For a nine-hour load, this is 21 students per class on the average instead of the 15.6 of the 1960s.

All these load figures are based on the typical two-semester arrangement of about 16.5 weeks each. Suppose, however, that our college worked on a different schedule. One such schedule might provide for a total of nine courses during the year, each to be taken one at a time for about three and one half to four weeks. The credit equivalent of each might be 3.5 semester hours. Each faculty member would teach one course, and each student would take one course. On the average, the class load would be sixteen students instead of twenty-one per class. At Colorado College this system is now in effect, and freedom exists on the number of hours classes meet. The average at Colorado is ten hours per week. Our college, under this system, would have weekly student-contact hours for faculty of 160 hours per week.

In this brief exercise we have accomplished the following for our college: leveled tuition off at $3,000; maintained a constant enrollment; increased the percentage of tuition income available for noncompensation purposes; doubled average total faculty compensation; reduced the total faculty 43 per cent; increased the average class size by 6 per cent and the number of weekly student-contact hours of faculty by 18 per cent; raised tuition 50 per cent.

There are many ways by which colleges can begin to *nurse themselves* back to better health. Even if financial problems continue to be chronic, as Professor William Bowen suggests they have been, they do not have to prove fatal. This exercise suggests only a partial cure, but since it deals with some of the vital aspects of the college—the faculty and the program—progress here can help the whole college to an early recovery.

CHAPTER 9

Cutting Instructional Costs

Howard R. Bowen,
Gordon K. Douglass

Since about 1955, American higher education has enjoyed an almost unbroken period of prosperity and advancement. Educators have been able to devote their energies to building, strengthening, and improving their institutions. This boom has abruptly come to an end. The problem now is to meet mounting deficits and even to keep the doors open. The thoughts of college administrators are therefore turning toward retrenchment and cost cutting. Everyone has on his mind the agonizing problem of how to make the budget balance without losing the hard-won educational gains of the past fifteen years.

One approach to solving the problem is to improve operating efficiency. This paper is a report on a study of how instruction might be organized in a liberal-arts college to reduce cost while maintaining or even improving quality.

There are many allegations that higher education is

ponderous, tradition-bound, unimaginative, and lacking in incentives to efficiency. Some observers hold that educational costs per student could be quickly reduced by one quarter or even one half if the principles of business management were applied. We have grave doubts about any such claims. Many of the allegations about inefficiency advocate assembly-line methods of instruction that would be educationally disastrous. Few of the people making such assertions would send *their* children to the kinds of colleges they are recommending. At the same time, we believe that most colleges and universities have not had strong incentives to improve efficiency, that they are staunchly resistant to change, and that improvements in efficiency might—over a period of years—offset a modest part of rising costs. We believe, moreover, that these gains in cost effectiveness might be achieved without any sacrifice in quality and possibly with improvement in quality.

Efficiency is measured as a ratio between two variables: cost and output. One of the problems in raising educational efficiency is that the outputs, which are in the form of changes in the lives of people, are extraordinarily difficult to measure. One's estimate of efficiency must be based on relatively subjective judgments about outcomes. We have not hesitated to make such subjective judgments, but we do not impose them upon anyone else. Each reader is free to make his own evaluations.

Sometimes it is argued that to raise educational efficiency one needs only to raise the teaching loads of professors. We do not deny that in certain isolated cases upward adjustments in teaching loads may be indicated. However, on the basis of our special studies of faculty work loads, we believe that a preponderant majority of faculty members are working at full capacity in relation, for example, to the effort of comparable professional people and executives. We also believe that college professors have major responsibilities for scholarship, research, public service, and institutional service, as well as for teaching, and that the success of their teaching in the long run depends on their having the opportunity and encouragement to participate professionally aside from instruction. Thus, although we will examine the effects of changes in teaching loads upon cost, we are not proposing an academic "stretch-out," in which so-called efficiency is achieved by increasing the hours worked by the professor or by shifting some of his energies from research and service to instruction.

Along the same line, we believe that good liberal education involves more than the transmission of facts and ideas of a kind that can be measured by test scores. It also involves outlooks, attitudes, values, motives, and development of character and personality. Therefore, it must include significant human and personal relationships between students and faculty and among students. We do not accept the concept that liberal education can be defined as an accumulation of credits or can be conveyed wholly by mechanical or assembly-line techniques. Nevertheless, we believe that efficiency can be improved— improved without loading the professor unduly and without neglecting the personal aspects of good liberal education.

Method of Investigation

Our study was based on simulation techniques. We created a hypothetical liberal-arts college with certain assumed characteristics and computed the costs of instruction with teaching conducted in a conventional manner (lecture-discussion, lecture-laboratory, and lecture-studio classes). Using these calculated costs as standards for comparison, we then modified various assumptions relating to such items as faculty teaching loads, curricular proliferation, plant utilization, and total enrollment and computed the effects on costs of these changes. Finally, we assumed various changes in the mode or system of instruction and computed their effects on costs.

The following instructional systems (in addition to the Conventional Plan) were considered: modification of the Conventional Plan by introducing a few lecture courses of large enrollment (a variant of the Ruml Plan); programmed independent study of a type that would require minimal time of the instructor and minimal specialized equipment other than library books; tutorial instruction (the Bakan Plan); programmed independent study using mechanical aids (the Kieffer Plan); and a plan of our own, combining these several methods. These plans represent the principal alternatives to conventional instruction and all are in use, at least experimentally, in many colleges.

The hypothetical college we used for our computations is roughly comparable in size and characteristics to Grinnell College or Pomona College, with which we happen to be familiar. For many of our assumptions we relied on a survey that we made of twenty liberal-arts colleges from all parts of the country. The hypothetical college has 1,200 students and 100 faculty members. The average faculty teaching load is two courses per semester for science teachers and two and a half courses for all others. Teachers devote on the average thirty hours a week during the academic year to instruction in all its aspects. Courses carry four credits, and the typical student load is four courses per semester. The average class size is twenty students. Faculty compensation averages $14,000 including fringes, with an additional allowance for the cost of such things as sabbaticals and sick leave. Physical-plant costs are calculated as a rental on required space with realistic assumptions about space utilization. Substantial sums are allocated to the library and computer facilities. The curriculum is considerably less proliferated than that actually found in most colleges of the type we surveyed.

Our effort to determine how the direct cost of instruction in this hypothetical college would be affected by variations in the way instruction is conducted was constrained by two conditions: first, that quality of education be maintained or improved; second, that faculty members not be expected to spend more than thirty hours a week during the academic year, or about 960 hours a year, on instruction—the remainder of their time being reserved for scholarly work, participation in the affairs of the college, and other professional activities.

Cost was expressed as total cost of instruction, cost per class offered, and cost per student course enrollment. The principal results of the calculations are shown in Tables 3 through 7.

Curricular Proliferation and Teaching Load

Table 3 shows the effect on instructional cost of variations in curricular proliferation and in faculty teaching loads under a conventional plan of instruction.

TABLE 3

COSTS OF CONVENTIONAL INSTRUCTION WITH VARYING
ASSUMPTIONS ABOUT CURRICULAR PROLIFERATION [a]
AND FACULTY TEACHING LOADS [b]

	Total Annual Instructional Cost	Cost per Class Offered	Cost per Student Course Enrollment
HIGHLY PROLIFERATED CURRICULUM			
Heavy teaching load	$2,332,000	$4,092	$243
Moderate teaching load	2,683,000	4,707	280
Light teaching load	3,206,000	5,623	334
MODERATELY PROLIFERATED CURRICULUM			
Heavy teaching load	1,985,000	4,170	208
Moderate teaching load	2,280,000 [c]	4,789 [c]	240 [c]
Light teaching load	2,714,000	5,702	285
COMPRESSED (LOW-PROLIFERATION) CURRICULUM			
Heavy teaching load	1,430,000	4,468	149
Moderate teaching load	1,628,000	5,087	170
Light teaching load	1,923,000	6,009	200

[a] *Highly proliferated:* 450 courses offered; 570 different classes; average class enrollment 17. *Moderately proliferated:* 335 courses offered; 476 different classes; average class enrollment 20. *Low proliferation:* 225 courses offered; 320 different classes; average class enrollment 30.

[b] *Heavy teaching load:* six lecture-discussion classes or five laboratory or studio classes per year. *Moderate load:* five lecture-discussion classes or four laboratory or studio classes per year. *Light load:* four lecture-discussion classes or three laboratory or studio classes per year.

[c] Standard plan used as base for comparison.

The highly proliferated curriculum, with 450 courses annually, is similar to that in many actual colleges. The compressed curriculum is based on two assumptions: (1) that only those subjects are offered (eighteen in all) which are common to virtually all good liberal-arts colleges; (2) that the number of courses in each subject is limited by what a panel of experienced professors in each field regards as the minimal number of courses needed for an adequate program. The professors indicated on the average that about 11 courses per field are needed. Multiplying 11 courses per field by 18 fields gives a total of 198 courses. To this total we added 27 courses to allow for some interdisciplinary courses and some flexibility, making the grand total 225 courses. The moderately proliferated curriculum is between the extremes.

The faculty teaching load ranges from heavy, which is really an ordinary three-course load per semester, to light, which is a two-course load.

The middle item in Table 3—moderately proliferated curriculum and moderate teaching load—is the standard upon which all of our cost comparisons are based.

In this table one can see the marked effect on cost of changes in teaching load and changes in curriculum. The variation is from $149 per student course enrollment to $334. With constant (moderate) teaching load, the variation is from $170 to $280.

Classroom Utilization and Enrollment

Table 4 makes similar comparisons for classroom utilization and total enrollment assuming a moderately proliferated curriculum and a moderate teaching load. The table shows that classroom space is so small a part of total cost that variations in classroom utilization exert little leverage on cost per student. These figures tend to answer the many critics of higher education who look upon improvement in space utilization as a panacea.

On the other hand, dramatic changes in cost are possible by increasing the total enrollment, *provided* the size of

TABLE 4

COST OF CONVENTIONAL INSTRUCTION WITH VARYING
ASSUMPTIONS ABOUT CLASSROOM UTILIZATION AND
NUMBERS OF STUDENTS

	Total Annual Instructional Cost	Cost per Class Offered	Cost per Student Course Enrollment
CLASSROOM UTILIZATION [a] (moderately proliferated curriculum; moderate teaching load)			
Intense	$2,248,000	$4,721	$236
Moderate	2,280,000 [b]	4,789 [b]	240 [b]
Low	2,312,000	4,856	244
NUMBERS OF STUDENTS (moderately proliferated curriculum; moderate teaching load)			
Student body of 1,200 (average class size 20)	2,280,000 [b]	4,789 [b]	240 [b]
Student body of 1,800 (average class size 30)	2,456,000	3,159	172

[a] *Intense utilization:* 37 hours per week, lecture-discussion class-rooms; 27 hours per week, science and fine-arts classrooms; 22 hours per week, studios and laboratories. *Moderate:* 25, 18, and 15 hours per week, respectively. *Low:* 18, 13, and 11 hours per week, respectively.

[b] Standard plan used as base for comparison.

faculty and curriculum is held constant. Usually, however, when colleges grow, the potential gains in efficiency are dissipated in multiplication of courses and staff.

Distribution of Faculty and Courses

Table 5 suggests that rank distribution of faculty and distribution of courses by subject are, within normal limits, not high-leverage variables, though of course changes in them do make an appreciable difference.

TABLE 5

COSTS OF CONVENTIONAL INSTRUCTION WITH VARYING
ASSUMPTIONS ABOUT RANK DISTRIBUTION OF FACULTY
AND COURSE DISTRIBUTION BY SUBJECTS

	Total Annual Instructional Cost	Cost per Class Offered	Cost per Student Course Enrollment
RANK DISTRIBUTION OF FACULTY [a] (moderately proliferated curriculum; moderate teaching load)			
Top-heavy	$2,338,000	$4,910	$246
Average (in twenty-college sample)	2,280,000 [b]	4,789 [b]	240 [b]
Bottom-heavy	2,035,000	4,275	214
COURSE DISTRIBUTION BY SUBJECTS (moderately proliferated curriculum; moderate teaching load)			
Average (in twenty-college sample)	2,280,000 [b]	4,789 [b]	240 [b]
Ten per cent reduction in number of more costly courses and correspondingly more of less expensive types	2,251,000	4,729	236

[a] *Top-heavy:* 64 per cent associate professors and professors; average compensation, $14,610. *Average:* 52 per cent associate professors and professors; average compensation, $14,000. *Bottom-heavy:* 30 per cent associate professors and professors; average compensation, $11,750.
[b] Standard plan used as base for comparison.

Minimal Cost

To see how low instructional costs could be pushed we looked at the Conventional Plan—with a compressed curriculum, heavy faculty teaching load, bottom-heavy rank distribution of faculty, intensive classroom utilization, and a mix of courses weighted toward less expensive subjects—and found that the cost per student enrollment would be only $127. With the addition of the Ruml Plan, this would be reduced still further to $117, which is less than half the standard figure of $240. The instructional budget of a college of 1,200 students employing all of these cost-cutting methods would be only $1,126,000.

Comparison of Three Instructional Plans

In Table 6, we compare the cost of three instructional plans that are alternatives to the conventional method of teaching-learning.

TABLE 6

COST OF INSTRUCTION UNDER THREE DIFFERENT PLANS:
PROGRAMMED INDEPENDENT STUDY, TUTORIAL (BAKAN
PLAN), AND INDEPENDENT STUDY WITH MECHANICAL
AIDS (KIEFFER PLAN)

	Total Annual Instructional Cost	Cost per Class Offered	Cost per Student Course Enrollment
PROGRAMMED INDEPENDENT STUDY PLAN			
Moderately proliferated curriculum	$2,138,000	$4,491	$225
Compressed curriculum	1,999,000	n.a.	207
Conventional Plan (for comparison)	2,280,000	4,789	240
TUTORIAL INSTRUCTION (BAKAN PLAN)	2,196,000 [a]	5,480	261 [a]
INDEPENDENT STUDY WITH LEARNING STATIONS AND MECHANICAL AIDS (KIEFFER PLAN)			
Moderately proliferated curriculum	2,636,000	5,537	277
Compressed curriculum	2,177,000	n.a.	227

[a] Total costs are lower than for the Conventional Plan, but cost per student course enrollment is higher because the Bakan Plan requires students to enroll in fewer courses during the junior and senior years.

Programmed Independent Study. The essence of the Programmed Independent Study Plan is that a fourth to a third of all courses are conducted through independent study. Each course uses a carefully devised program that can be followed by many students on roughly the same time schedule. The program is outlined initially in a syllabus that suggests readings; assigns papers, problems, and operations; and schedules examinations. At an initial meeting, the instructor of each course makes clear, however, that within the broad framework of the course each student has considerable latitude to pursue his own interests through research and original writing. Students are free to consult the instructor individually about their projects, and the instructor meets from time to time with the entire class for discussion. But the course is managed so that the instructor spends considerably less time in all the course's activities than he would ordinarily spend on a conventional course. Students, instead, replace the instructor as the sources of some instructional inputs.

This plan can be combined with supervised laboratory instruction, or it can include some activity at "learning stations" where mechanized learning aids are available. With these modifications, the plan would be adaptable to most subjects.

As Table 6 shows, the savings under this plan would not be spectacular. The average cost would be $225, as compared with $240 under a purely conventional plan. However, our calculations indicate that this plan is economically feasible, and our judgment is that it is educationally desirable.

Tutorial Instruction. Next we examined tutorial instruction, using as our model a plan suggested by David Bakan.[1] This plan arranges the instructional system so that the tutorial method can be achieved without undue cost. At the beginning of each term, each student develops an individualized study plan with the instructor of each of his courses. Normally he enrolls in four courses per semester during the freshman and sophomore years, and three per semester during the junior and

[1] "Plan for a College," *Canadian University and College,* June 1969, pp. 30–34, 42, 43.

senior years. Instructors have wide flexibility in the conduct of their courses but meet their students individually in tutorials at least three times (preferably more) during a semester—once to agree on course assignments and requirements, once to review the students' progress, and once to evaluate their accomplishments. Instructors can also meet their students from time to time in lecture-discussion classes.

It would be possible for instructors to meet all their students individually for one hour every two weeks without exceeding the thirty hours a week that each instructor is expected to devote to instruction. The number of tutorials could be increased even more if the length of time of each individual conference were shortened or if more than one student attended each tutorial session. It would not be difficult to arrange a weekly half-hour tutorial session for every student in each course.

The interesting feature of the Bakan Plan is that it demonstrates the feasibility of incorporating tutorial instruction into a college program without raising the work load of instructors (assuming that thirty hours a week during the academic year is a reasonable amount of time for a faculty member to devote to instruction).

From the point of view of efficiency, the Bakan Plan would not reduce instructional costs, but neither would it necessarily raise them. The particular variant we selected for study would cost $261 per student, as compared with $240 for a purely conventional plan. We could easily have manipulated the curriculum and the number of tutorials offered to bring the cost down to the $240 standard.

Independent Study with Mechanical Aids. The next plan we considered was one involving extensive use of mechanical learning aids, as proposed by Dr. Jarold A. Kieffer of Macalester College.[2] This mode of instruction calls for courses in which, with the assistance of modern teaching-learning equipment and willing instructors, students can study

[2] "Toward a System of Individually Taught Courses," *Liberal Education,* October 1970.

at their own convenience and at their own pace. Each course has a program organized in sequential phases. The program consists of instructions, reading assignments, problems, use of audio-visual materials when relevant, laboratory tasks, field trips, the witnessing of demonstrations, and performing of various operations. For some courses (for instance, laboratory science courses) procedures might differ little from conventional course work. For others (such as English literature or history) the program consists primarily of reading, problem solving, and writing, and might be centered on the library. For many courses, however, special "learning stations," containing programmed course materials, are provided. At these stations students individually can view and hear materials continuously, in segments, or repeatedly, through manipulation of simple controls.

For a typical course, each student comes at his convenience to a learning station (or library or laboratory if that is the station) and works on the program for Phase I of the course at his own pace. At the completion of the phase he, along with other students in the same state of readiness, attends a seminar with the course instructor. Each seminar provides informal discussion, opportunities for questions and answers, and additional perspective. After this, if the student judges that he is ready, he takes a test. If he passes the test, he proceeds to Phase II. If he fails, he returns to Phase I, with no penalty other than delay, to repair his deficiencies. A comprehensive examination after successful completion of all phases is the basis of the course grade, although the results of reports, reading, or term papers can also be counted. The student is free at any time during the course to consult his instructor privately, but their primary contact is in seminars and indirectly at learning stations, where programmed learning materials bear the unmistakable mark of each instructor.

The Kieffer Plan, like the preceding two plans, is based on independent study. It differs from other plans, however, in the heavy commitment of time each Kieffer Plan instructor must make in preparing and updating programs and in the heavy investment in equipment and purchased software.

Clearly, the Kieffer Plan admits of great variations in cost per student, depending on the amount of equipment needed, the number of students involved, and other variables. The specific plan that we selected, suitable to a liberal-arts college, would cost $277 a student as compared with the standard $240 for conventional instruction—suggesting that programmed independent study based on mechanized equipment is at least within range of reasonable cost. If one were willing to trade off some curricular proliferation to buy some Kieffer Plan courses, the cost might drop to $227, as shown at the bottom of Table 6.

Recommended Eclectic Plan

Finally, Table 7 presents the results of our experimentation with an eclectic plan, which we recommend on both

TABLE 7

COSTS OF INSTRUCTION UNDER AN ECLECTIC PLAN

	Total Annual Instructional Cost	Cost per Class Offered	Cost per Student Course Enrollment
STANDARD ECLECTIC PLAN [a]			
Highly proliferated curriculum	$2,361,000	$5,401	$246
Moderately proliferated curriculum	2,036,000	5,593	212
Compressed curriculum	1,576,000	6,345	164
MINIMUM-COST ECLECTIC PLAN [b]	1,288,000	5,214	134
CONVENTIONAL PLAN (for comparison)	2,280,000	4,789	240

[a] Assumes 35 per cent of instruction in Conventional Plan classes, Ruml Plan 25 per cent, programmed independent study 15 per cent, Kieffer Plan 10 per cent, and Bakan Plan 15 per cent.

[b] Compressed curriculum; heavy faculty teaching load; bottom-heavy rank distribution of faculty; intensive classroom utilization; mix of courses weighted toward less expensive subjects.

educational and economic grounds. Under this plan, 35 per cent of the instruction is given in the conventional manner, 25 per cent by Rumlized large lectures, 15 per cent by programmed independent study, 10 per cent by mechanized independent study, and 15 per cent by tutorials.

We believe there is value in providing varied educational experiences. We also believe that American higher education should depart from its heavy reliance on conventional, closely supervised, teacher-oriented instruction. A varied plan including large elements of independent study is called for.

As shown in Table 7, our eclectic plan is significantly less costly than the Conventional Plan—$212 per student, as compared with $240—and the cost could be reduced to as low as $134 with simplification of the curriculum and other changes mentioned in the table.

We believe that there is a bright future for the kind of independent study that increases a student's self-reliance and that requires and equips him to learn independently with a minimum of dependence upon instructors.

Our main conclusions are that there is ample opportunity within prevailing economic constraints for bold educational experimentation. A corollary is that faculty discussions of educational policy should be more attuned to budgetary considerations than they have been traditionally. The curriculum, the mode of instruction, and the teaching load do make a difference in costs. They may not spell the difference between institutional solvency and bankruptcy, but they may make the difference between institutional progress and stagnation.

CHAPTER 10

Student Services

G. Wayne Glick

The most important state-
ment made in any presentation is the first statement—there the
context is set.[1] So I will announce a text, which we shall cir-
cumambulate and to which we shall return at the end. That
text: "A society that does not listen to its poets will have to
listen to its generals." You may ask, fairly: "What does *that*
have to do with student services viewed from a cost point of
view? Are you not charged to comment on the fiscal management of health services, counseling, student unions, financial
aid, placement, and alumnae?" Yes. Knowing what I am sup-
posed to do, I will seem to do something else before coming to
the specific charge.

Let me, by means of quotations, say some things that
seem to me important as to context.

Robert Nisbet, Professor of Sociology at the University

---

[1] I want to acknowledge the considerable help given me by Earl
Bloomquist, the director of institutional research at Keuka College, in the
preparation of this paper.

of California at Riverside, has the following grim prediction about the future of the university in our society:

> Great societies and periods of history have existed before in human history without universities; they certainly can again. Despite the well-sown myth of the university's indispensability to our technologically advanced society, there are other, existing sources of such knowledge needing only to be developed and multiplied. . . . What the university in America had to offer was not unique manufacture of knowledge, but a unique structure of authority resident in a unique intellectual community. Very little else.

My second setting of context comes from the December 13, 1970, issue of *The New York Times,* containing a story on a survey conducted by the American Civil Liberties Union:

> An American Civil Liberties Union survey of 155 college presidents indicates a steady extension of civil liberties to students and a corresponding decline of the colleges' and universities' practice of functioning as surrogate parents.
> The survey showed increasing student participation in college governance, more protection of students' constitutional rights as citizens, and a substantial improvement in their right to arrange their own personal lives.[2]

Finally, let me quote from an article written by Chad Walsh entitled "If You Would Know the Young, Look to Their Poets."

> In the poetry most loved by students, whether written by their peers or their elders, two sets of themes predominate. First there are poems on the need to relate and the difficulties in doing so; love; the quest for identity; the masquerades and deceptions. . . .
> . . . To the new poetry public, what a poem says is more important than technical details of form. The key requirements are "relevance," "sincerity." That one poet

[2] M. S. Handler, "Gain by Students on Rights Found," *New York Times,* December 13, 1970, p. 62.

is excellent and another is not matters little. They are appreciated as preachers and philosophers, not as creators of aesthetic perfections. . . .

The young, with their poetry readings and Woodstocks, are demanding respect for intuition, emotion, the whole dark and teeming vitality of the archetypal unconscious. Most of all, they are demanding a society in which people are persons, not personnel.

The university is not indispensable; its functions *in loco parentis* are atrophying; students demand to be treated as persons, not personnel; yet such is the financial status of higher education that student services must also be evaluated coldly from a fiscal point of view.

No college today can ignore the mixture of financial, moral, and traditional questions that relate to student services that I will be raising in this essay; but two fundamental questions stand apart: Should a college—can a college?—seek to provide a total range of services, as a microcosm of the culture; or must it deliberately limit student services of an extra-academic sort? Another question that will be dealt with directly is the matter of student expectations, particularly at a time when students are asking for and being granted a higher degree of participation in the governance process.

One of the most provocative articles on my desk from the *NASPA Journal* for January 1970 is entitled simply: "Will Student Personnel Work Survive the 70s?" If that is a dour question, consider that Nisbet and others are asking an even graver question: "Will colleges and universities survive the 70s?" If they do—this is my argument—they will have to deal far more creatively with an emerging student ethos, and this creativity must show itself in all particular student services. Let us come then to the various specific "student services," raising questions in the context I have just described.

Health Service

An article contained in *The Chronicle of Higher Education* for April 27, 1970, reports on the Fifth National Conference on Health in College Communities, held in Boston, at which student expectation was made very clear.

> Besides providing day-to-day medical care, college health services—called student health centers or infirmaries on some campuses—must turn their attention to improving the total mental and physical health of their campus communities, including the campus environment affecting that health. . . .
> Health services' concerns with the campus environment, one of the reports said, should involve "not only the obvious physical hazards, but also those sources of emotional and social stress which distort human relationships." . . .
> A task force on the "ecology of health" said campus problems that ought to concern health services include the competitive nature of education, campus governance and administration, food and food services, chemicals used in laboratories and cleaning, noise, crowding of classes and dormitories, pollution of the physical environment of the campus, and depersonalization of students. . . .[8]

The article also discusses students' demands that they have a voice in running health services and their complaints that these services are too impersonal.

Can a college, today, deliver on this kind of student expectation? Clearly, students—and parents—feel that the college has something of a *total* responsibility. So far as the particular elements of this responsibility are concerned, a list can be well nigh limitless: some say that a college health service should take responsibility for long-term treatment; most say that it is a duty of a college to provide drug information and treatment; many say that medication of all varieties should be available free; and there are increasing pressures on the college to provide birth-control information and devices—not to speak of the pressure for abortion information. How is a college to "manage" *fiscally* a health service of such total range?

[8] P. W. Semas, "Preventive Approach Urged on College Health Services," *Chronicle of Higher Education*, April 27, 1970, p. 12.

Counseling

We see also a rising student expectation and demand for counseling services: psychological, academic, and personal counseling, and in some cases institutional involvement in family and personal problems. During the last decade these services in colleges have expanded greatly, but the demand has not abated. What this means for the management of a total institution in a time of rising financial emergency is so patent it hardly needs to be spelled out. However, to make the point, let me use an illustration from the college I serve. In the course of the six years that I have been at Keuka College, we have moved from a "psychiatrist on call" plus a part-time personal counselor plus the "usual" faculty advising system, *through* a period of a full-time counseling psychologist and a carefully developed academic advising system and an expanded staff to deal with personal counseling, *to* a present situation in which the academic advising system remains, the personal counseling capability remains, but the psychological counseling is done by a nearby university psychologist at one fourth the cost of the full-time counseling psychologist. My point is that at this moment we are providing adequate if not optimal counseling, and doing it at considerably less cost than was true two years ago. And we have had to do this because of fiscal stringency, so widely documented in various studies, preeminently in the study carried out by William Jellema of the Association of American Colleges.

Student Unions

Questions that might be raised about student unions, in addition to those broader questions that we have already mentioned, include the following: Who should supervise student unions—students or staff members? Should bookstores and snack bars run deficits or should they make money? If the latter, should all income produced from these auxiliary services be placed in scholarships, or is this simply an administrative fiction? When we ask the question "Who should run the student union?" do we thereby mean that students alone might deter-

mine policies; if so, what is the relation of the student governing group to the administration and the trustees of the college?

Financial Aid

Coming from a college that has increased its financial
aid to students over a five-year period by 350 per cent, I have
some sensitivity to the range of problems connected with this
area of institutional administration. Let me list some of the
questions that have arisen in our own case. What is the break-
ing point in a budget when financial aid increases so dramatically? Should financial aid be used solely as a recruiting tool
(as a lure for any student—neither bright nor needy necessarily
—who won't come without it), or as an aid to bright students
or as aid to needy students? Does the disadvantaged student
really have a chance for aid? What renewal policies should be
in effect? Who exercises control over student aid—a faculty
committee or an administrative officer? What is the prognosis
in the 1970s for federal aid in this area? Will the 1970s require
more aid for the middle-class student?

Another question is increasingly being asked in this area,
a question that George Schlekat[4] has put sharply: "Do Financial-Aid Programs Have a Social Conscience?" More precisely he
asks: "Does the social background of an applicant for college
financial aid affect the treatment his application receives from
college aid administrators? More specifically, do college financial-aid programs discriminate among students of different
socioeconomic classes in deciding whether to award aid and
what types and amounts of aid to award?" A clue to some of
the answers to these questions is provided in a recent study
by the College Board's College Scholarship Service, as reported
by Schlekat. Parents' confidential statements filed for the 1965–
66 academic year revealed definite differences in treatment,
with favor afforded to both lower-class and upper-class applicants—the former because of poverty, the latter because of
superior test scores. Lower-class applicants seemed to have a

[4] G. A. Schlekat, "Do Financial-Aid Programs Have a Social Conscience?" *College Board Review*, Fall 1968, *69*, 15–20.

better chance of receiving awards; these awards, however, were accompanied by repayable loans and required the student to work, while upper-class applicants were receiving outright grants.

A further clue toward bias was reflected recently in a test given to children. One question asked, "What would you do if you were sent to the store to buy a loaf of bread and the grocer said that he was out of bread?" The *only* answer that received credit was: "I would go to another store"; the child from a ghetto area who answered "I would go home" received no credit. Presumably, in the ghetto area, there was only one store and no transportation was available to travel any distance to another store.

Placement

When we come to the subject of placement, we encounter student expectancy with a vengeance. Everyone knows that the job market generally is worse than it has been for years. With this fact—usually not taken into account by students—there has come a greater clamor for colleges to provide placement services that will, supposedly, guarantee that students will get positions. Admittedly, this has resulted in part from the *in loco parentis* stance of American higher education—expanded to the *n*th degree in the sixties, to the point of "coddling" the students. Should employment counseling be a responsibility of the college? What are the trends in corporate and business recruitment? To what degree can a college provide placement counseling for a student who does not have a commitment to any specific vocation? And, as an omnibus question, does an institution really have the option of declaring itself out of this particular area?

It is a relatively easy matter for an institution to determine the cost of placement services in dollars. What is far more difficult, if not impossible, is the determination of success or failure of such a program. A "success-oriented" society intrudes pressures (economic, social, political) which often overwhelm individuals. Is a corporation executive more "successful" than a poet? Some insist that a graduate "well placed" is in itself a mark of success of the program; others argue that if the educational process has not enabled a person to "be human," then no matter how "well placed" a person is, education has failed.

Alumni

Let me simply list here several questions that must be faced in the management of this particular area of a college's activity. Are alumni affairs basically fund-raising operations or public relations efforts? Can alumni be kept informed of the rapid changes of the 1970s without extensive public relations budgets? What can a college offer alumni as authentic services rather than contrived rah-rah functions? Should alumni run their own affairs, or should alumni programs be centered at the college? To what degree should an institution regard the student body as "alumni" from the moment they set foot on the campus as freshmen? How, if this is a desirable expectation, can students be cultivated so as to become supportive alumni?

Conclusion

It is no secret that most of the small colleges of the country are facing financial pressures of a sort they have not known in a decade. These comments therefore center around this particular phenomenon as it relates to student services.

No college can afford all the student services desired, and therefore the preparation of a budget must become a weighing of value judgments concerning equitable deployment of the resources of an institution. Although it may seem simplistic and harsh to suggest that the institution cannot afford any student service that does not pay its own way, it is now an elemental fact of life for most institutions. Students who know and understand this will, on their own, make adjustments to compensate for loss of services.

In budget preparation student services must be seen as a part of the totality of a budget and not be given a *sui generis* status. In other words, institutional priorities must be carefully and constantly assessed in order to maintain a balance that is responsive to the purpose of the institution and to its genuine needs. Thus, even though a *sui generis* status for student services is not desirable, an institution must establish priorities within the context of its purpose and the needs of persons. When a student service serves the well-being of the student, it ultimately serves the academic purposes of the institution. Any refinement of priorities after that is a matter for each institution to determine. Elements that would influence that refinement would include the size and location of the institution, the nature of the student body, the complexity of the community in which the institution exists, availability of persons for specialized services, attitudes of the college community, and fund resources or limitations.

A "true cost" picture of every student service subsidized by an institution must be gained. Much more sophisticated cost analysis is necessary than that presently being used. In their *Cost Accounting*,[5] Adolph Matz, Othel J. Curry, and George W. Frank have identified at least seventeen modifiers of "cost": direct, prime, indirect, fixed, variable, controllable, product, joint, estimated, standard, future, replacement, opportunity, imputed, sunk, differential, and out-of-pocket. The Western Interstate Commission for Higher Education (WICHE) through its National Center for Higher Education Management Systems is providing information, models, and procedures to help institutions make accurate analyses. Colleges must "get with it" in assessing *all* costs and conducting this assessment openly and by means of proven methodologies.

More attention should be given to the possibility of contracting certain services to extra-campus groups. The range here is almost inexhaustible: securing outside faculty to teach in specialized summer programs, catering services to host conference groups, offering programs for underachievers who may be prospective students, contracting health services to nearby hospitals or health agencies (where possible), a much broader use of public services, where available—these illustrate possibilities colleges should explore.

Long-range planning is essential if the implications of

[5] A. Matz, O. J. Curry, and G. W. Frank, *Cost Accounting* (2nd ed.) (Cincinnati: South-Western, 1957).

a given expenditure are to be adequately assessed. Here Sidney
Tickton's *Letter to a College President* [6] provides a clue in
posing the questions, the answers to which form the context
for all long-range planning. What population changes for the
country as a whole, and by categories of the population, may be
expected? What does this suggest to an institution about training the labor force? What is the economic outlook for college
and university enrollments, particularly for private institutions? If higher education is expected to cost more, can the
country afford it?

What about student participation in the determination
of institutional priorities and management objectives? The
Linowitz Committee on Campus Tensions makes the following
recommendations: students should be given substantial autonomy in nonacademic and curricular affairs; students cannot be
shielded from the consequences of their behavior when it vio-
lates the laws of society; colleges should review with legal
counsel their practices regarding confidentiality of information
about students and the privacy of student living quarters; students should be informed about the institution's decision-
making process; students should recognize and respect the
rights and privileges of their fellow students; students must be
encouraged to practice voluntary self-discipline; and students
and administrators have equal rights and responsibilities in
proposing educational changes. [7]

Finally, let me play the very dangerous game of prophet,
making guesses about the 1970s as they relate to the student. I
would guess at the outset that the surprises in store for us will
go far beyond the imagination of any of us. Whether they extend as far as Mr. Nisbet has suggested, I would not guess; but
I think it a real possibility, perhaps a probability, that the
"received structure" of American higher education will be
drastically changed in this decade. Let me illustrate this by
harking back to the question about the range of services that

[6] S. Tickton, *Letter to a College President* (New York: Fund for the
Advancement of Education, 1963), p. 9.

[7] "Linowitz Panel's Recommendations on College Unrest," *Chronicle
of Higher Education,* April 27, 1970, pp. 3–6.

ought to be provided by small liberal-arts colleges. Our answer until recently has been "More and more services." My guess is that the future answer to this question might come out somewhat as follows: *The students themselves will become less interested in our complex "style of life" and will be less and less responsive to the "full range of services" approach.*

I take direct issue here with those who see the post-Cambodia quiet on American campuses as meaning that the students have decided to be good children after all, and therefore we can proceed with business as usual. In this regard, the record of the academic prophets has been something less than brilliant. In the summer of 1969 the presidents were saying that the worst was past. The campuses exploded in the spring of 1970. In the summer of 1970 the presidents were saying that they expected more and more trouble. The campuses, in 1971, were veritable pools of stagnation. Inevitably, there has been a cacophony of voices taking credit for "a firm stand in putting the students in their places." Nonsense! The students have simply shown that they are able to outwit any predicting administrator.

But I hope I am saying more than this. I believe the revolution in which we are involved is so elemental and profound that the bases on which our predictions are made will simply no longer serve as a *sole* basis. The simplistic analysis presently going on on many campuses—referring to the student generation as indulging in a "new romanticism" as an antithesis to rationalism—is shallow and fruitless. Margaret Mead is correct when she draws the analogy of the young generation as natives of a country in which we old folks are the immigrants. We shall be prepared to provide leadership of value only, I think, as we assimilate this fact into the daily operation of our colleges—even in the mundane areas of student services. What this will mean practically will be determined partly by local situation, but mainly by a cultural *Geist* which is running very strongly indeed. Certainly few of the nostrums of the past will suffice. For the kids know in their bones—maybe it's the mercury or the strontium 90 working—that the age of nations is past. It is time to listen to the poets and to rebuild the earth.

PART IV

SPECIAL PROBLEMS
OF PRIVATE
INSTITUTIONS

To ask whether private higher education has a future is an alarming, not an alarmist, question. There is real reason today for doubting that private institutions can long continue to play a viable and meaningful role in higher education. Although these institutions have not yet ceased to grow, their growth rate has slowed to a fraction of 1 per cent per annum, and their share of the total enrollment is only half what it was twenty years ago.

Percentages, however, tell the least significant things about the situation. What is paramount is the diversity and quality of the educational program. Private higher education must exhibit a qualitative difference in its purpose or program, or it will have little to contribute to the rest of higher education and little to offer potential students by way of a choice. This, in turn, will aggravate the fiscal condition that already makes it difficult to maintain a qualitative difference

All institutions of higher learning—private and tax- supported—suffer from similar problems in finance, in management, in communication with and support by constituencies. However, some facets of these problems have sharper edges for private institutions than for tax-supported ones. A decline to mediocrity for a prestigious public institution would be grievous but not the catastrophe that it would be for a private institution. It is much more likely that the question of bare survival would be raised in the latter instance than in the former.

Educators in predominately tax-supported institutions may, in some instances, be forgiven if they indulge in some ephemeral pleasure over the ascendancy of their own institutions and the decline of private institutions; but this pleasure must be short term. Public higher education needs strong private higher education. Without private institutions to demonstrate the meaning of independence in higher education, public institutions may experience a steady attrition of the degree of autonomy they presently enjoy. Private colleges and universities share with private institutions generally the responsibility for standing as buffers between the individual and the corporate state and for establishing a comparable role for tax-supported institutions. That is why the financial health of private higher education is important. If the means to support these institutions—which are necessary for giving expression to constitutional freedoms—are unattainable, those freedoms themselves may be in jeopardy.

In the papers that follow, *William W. Jellema* outlines the dimensions of the contemporary financial situation in private higher education, *Sharvy G. Umbeck* suggests ways to pursue fresh sources of income, and *Dennis L. Johnson* makes recommendations for an aggressive admissions program. The private college must have students as well as money. It is left to *Howard R. Bowen* to ask—and to answer optimistically—the question basic to this section: "Does private higher education have a future?"

CHAPTER 11

Financial Status

William W. Jellema

The first sketches for the depressing financial picture of private higher education—sketches revealing steadily rising costs, a slowly widening tuition gap between public and private higher education, an expansion of student services, mounting inflation, and a declining rate of enrollment—were drawn before 1968. The fiscal year 1968, however, became for us a "base year," because it was then that we began to collect income and expenditure data for a financial study of private higher education. So it may be useful to say something about the kind of year 1968 was as a foundation for a study of this nature.

We were told, in an AAUP report for 1968, that faculty salaries had risen an average of $4,600 since 1956. We were also told, by William Baumol of Princeton, that real expenditures per student had increased 65 per cent (calculated in constant dollars) in private institutions of higher learning during the course of the decade ending with fiscal 1968. If the trend continued uncorrected, Professor Baumol prophesied, the cost per student in current dollars could rise in forty years to sixteen times the 1968 level.

A study conducted in the state of Texas, also in 1968, indicated that if the short trend uncovered in that study were to continue, and if the percentage covered by tuition were the same in 1985 as in 1968, the student at a private university would be asked to pay $17,324 per year.

In 1968 also, a friend sent me an excerpt from the annual report of a college president:

> During all the years of [our] development as a church-related university, [we have] experienced a great frequency of financial crises. Only the Almighty's repeated answering of the sustained prayers raised by the school's courageous board and administration has prevented many potential catastrophes from occurring. . . . Now, however, the seriousness of the commitments necessary to implement the university's ambitious program requires that the needed degree and continuity of support be more clearly defined and more definitely assured.

"Obviously," my informant commented, "things are in one hell of a mess!"

This, then, was the way the situation looked in 1968— the "base" year, and by far the best financial year, in our study. From that point, our data show, a bad situation has deteriorated rapidly. As Pogo might have said, looking at the following three years of financial data from the standpoint of 1968, "From here on down, it's all uphill."

In the years since, costs have continued to rise. Instruction costs are higher, with no increase in productivity; building costs are higher; maintenance costs are higher; security costs are higher; students and their parents are demanding "wall-to-wall" services; and inflation has continued to blur any kind of financial datum line.

If we look at net surplus or deficit for the current operating fund, the "average" institution (a gross statistical amalgam derived by dividing the total net surplus or deficit figure for all institutions in our study by the number of institutions) finished fiscal year 1968 with a surplus. One year later it finished its fiscal year with a *deficit*—which, it anticipated, it would *quintuple* one year later still, the fiscal year ending (for most institutions) June 30, 1970.

If we look at the "average" institution in each of nine geographical regions, however, a somewhat different picture emerges. The break between 1968 and 1969 does not appear as sharp. In some regions the average institution was already running a deficit in 1968; in other regions the decline into deficits was delayed for the average institution until 1970.

Specifically, in three regions, geographically separated from one another, the average institution ended fiscal year 1968 with a deficit. One year later, the average institution in three more regions finished the year with a deficit, and by the end of fiscal year 1970 the average institution in the remaining three regions ended with a deficit. Membership in the deficit club was complete: the average institution in every region was firmly in the red.

Statistically summarized and arranged in five enrollment-level categories, all private colleges and universities showed a steady decline in financial condition from 1967–68 through 1968–69 and 1969–70. By 1968–69, private colleges and universities in every enrollment-level category but one, taken as a statistical average, were showing a deficit—not a contrived "deficit," not an indirect student-aid "deficit" (which all private institutions have been running for years), not the kind of "deficit" administrators sometimes submit to their boards to stimulate giving, not the "deficit" sometimes reported before annual gift money or contributed services provided by a religious order are included as income, but *an actual current-fund deficit* much as you and I have when our total actual expenditures are larger than our total actual income.

Some individual institutions in each of these categories, of course, were running deficits in 1967–68 and even earlier; some institutions in each category continue to run surpluses; but the "average" institution in each of the five categories finished in the *black* in 1967–68 and, in every category but one, finished firmly in the *red* in 1968–69, one year later. So much for the good news.

Projection Game

One end of our four years of data was fixed to the year 1968. The other was pinned to 1970–71, a year whose fiscal fortune was not yet fact. These projected data are, perforce, spongy and uneven. The making of projections is a spooky enterprise. There seemed to be, however, a certain earthy reliability about a summation of predictions made at the local level. These predictions were affected by word from the admissions office; worries from the development office; intimations of still higher costs; speculation about the amount of tuition increase the local constituency would bear; rumors of the establishment or further development of a local junior college; grim decisions of where to cut back, in what order, and when—all compounded by hopes and fears concerning the national economy.

Some institutions overestimated the deficit they would incur. Others, a larger number, underestimated. For the second projected year an even larger number underestimated the deficits they would incur. Hope, a little inebriated by unwarranted optimism, seems to outrun despair in projecting future income. For example, some institutions that showed a stable or even declining amount of gifts and grants for the three years beginning in 1967–68 suddenly projected an astonishing increase in unrestricted gifts. Perhaps they thought they knew something that the reviewer of questionnaires did not; perhaps a highly favorable will was expected to be probated in that year. To one not privy to such inside information, the projection looked more like a desperate fiction invented to project a balanced budget.

Similar unrestrained enthusiasm is sometimes seen in the projection of tuition and fees. An institution that has been experiencing a decline in applications and enrollment may project a sudden increase in its freshman enrollment by some very large amount. For a given institution this is possible. *But not nationally.* There are simply not enough students available of the academic quality and financial ability that these colleges and universities have traditionally admitted to make such optimistic projections come true. It is both unreasonable and irresponsible to look at the total national scene and say, "If those colleges would just get off their duffs and go looking for students, they could eliminate their deficits." It simply is not so.

Financial projection patterns, however, are by no means identical, as the following comparison of two groups of institutions approximately equal in number will indicate.

The institutions (about fifty in the nation as a whole) that ran a relatively small deficit in 1968–69 had, typically, run a surplus the year before and projected a deficit for 1969–70 nearly nine times larger than the deficit they ran in 1968–69. For 1970–71 they projected a deficit only two thirds the size of the previous year's deficit. To call this an improvement in their financial condition is a little like calling a rise in temperature from ninety degrees below zero to sixty degrees below zero a "warming trend." Yet it is instructive to notice the basis for this relatively milder financial climate.

Almost all *expenditure items* in educational and general, as well as student aid and auxiliary enterprises, were projected by these institutions to *continue to rise*. The "warming trend" difference must therefore occur in income. But not in all income areas. These institutions projected actual declines in income for some items and hoped for no dramatic increases in any other areas save two: tuition income and gift and grant income. They projected a rise in unrestricted gift and grant income of 25 per cent for 1970–71, even though their income from this source had declined the previous year by nearly 6 per cent. Tuition and fee income is not quite as dramatic. Income from this source was projected to increase in 1970–71 over the previous year by 12 per cent, as that year had increased over the previous year by 11 per cent and that year in turn had shown an increase over 1967–68 by 12 per cent. What is dramatic is not the nearly 40 per cent increase in tuition income in 1970–71 over 1967–68, but the expectation of a continuing significant rise in tuition in view of the evidence of a declining pool of applicants for admission at those institutions.

However, as noted above, the institutions did not expect even these increases in income to redeem them from a deficit condition, but merely to introduce a warming breeze into their Antarctica of deficits.

By comparison, the approximately fifty institutions in the nation that in 1968–69 ran a larger deficit—between $100,000 and $150,000, as opposed to the institutions described above which ran a deficit less than $25,000—projected a similar trend line (that is, a deficit nearly eight times larger in 1969–70, followed by a projected improvement—which cuts the deficit in less than half—in 1970–71), but for quite different reasons.

Not a single income category was projected by this latter group of institutions to improve in 1970–71 over 1969–70. The reason for the milder deficit lies, in this case, in *reduced expenditures*. In every single current-fund expenditure item, these institutions expected to spend less than the year before—enough less, in fact, that they expected to incur a lesser deficit even though they also projected a declining income.

It appears that the latter group—those institutions with the larger deficit that expected to improve their financial position by reducing expenditures—are more realistic than the former group—those institutions with a smaller deficit that expected improvement by a marked rise in income. Perhaps the larger deficit has a more sobering effect on future planning.

Updating Projections

That the projections—grim though they were—were often based upon unwarranted optimism was confirmed in a follow-up study.[1] The average institution that expected a deficit in fiscal 1970 of $104,000 actually had a deficit of $131,000—26 per cent worse than anticipated. The updated projection for fiscal 1971 was for a deficit of $158,000—nearly *eight times the deficit* incurred by the average institution only two years earlier.

Even more depressing is the picture when examined region by region. In seven of the nine geographical regions, fiscal 1971 looked to be a year with deficits even more severe

[1] Available through ERIC Document Reproduction Service, National Cash Register Company, 4936 Fairmont Avenue, Bethesda, Maryland 20014.

than those of fiscal 1970. What is especially distressing is that a year earlier—the summer of 1970—the average institution in four regions had looked forward to an improved position and now faced still deeper deficits.

Behind these mounds of deficits, moreover, lie the broken remains of curtailed operations, of innovation untried, and of creativity curbed. If these cutbacks had not been made, the deficits must surely have been much higher.

If, in fiscal 1971, private colleges and universities run deficits no greater than they anticipated, 175 private colleges and universities will have exhausted or exceeded their total liquid assets. They can go no more years without plunging into debt—further into debt in most cases. If private institutions continue to run deficits of this magnitude, within the decade nearly half of them will have exhausted their total liquid assets. When these assets are gone, they become candidates for bankruptcy.

"Surplus" and "Deficit"

Since private higher education is frequently enough dealt with in terms that suggest something faintly venal and unscrupulous about the high and ever rising tuition such institutions charge, some may raise their eyebrows at the very notion of "surpluses" and liquid assets in a supposedly nonprofit institution. They may see no harm in trimming down an institution's "unappropriated surplus"—believing intuitively that a nonprofit institution should run a breakeven annual budget. A word of explanation may be in order.

There are *no stockholders* of accredited private institutions of higher learning to gather annually in person or by proxy to decide how to distribute the profits of their enterprise. There often are, however, surplus funds at the end of the year— if the economy is beneficial, the administration is efficient, and the public is supportive. A surplus at the end of a year's operation is an important source of growth capital which a college or university cannot count on getting, except by a special act of external benevolence, from other sources. It means that the institution can do the innovative and imaginative things the public has come to expect of it and which it does well. It can launch a new venture or strengthen one already begun. It can increase the amount of aid it offers to students in need. It can avoid an increase in tuition or, to meet constantly rising costs, make that increase a modest one.

All of these things a college cannot do if it runs a deficit or merely breaks even. An institution barely afloat, with water nearly over the gunwales, has lost much of its maneuverability, its adventurousness, and its freedom of experimentation. Its innovation and risk taking is confined to putting to sea each academic year. Most ominously, it has no protection against storms. A little student unrest, a little decline in enrollment, a little disenchantment among donors, and the ship may founder. The first thing it does in troubled financial seas is jettison cargo.

Meeting a Deficit

When confronted by a deficit, a college may do one or more of several things. The most popular reaction is to borrow —including from current funds—and to transfer from unappropriated surplus. These choices are conditioned, of course, by the availability of loan money and the rate at which it is available, as well as by the presence or absence of unappropriated surplus. A very large number of institutions have no "unappropriated surplus"—indeed, no liquid assets of any kind; and one hears rumors of others that are unable to borrow money.

Some institutions are under the delusion that they need do nothing about a deficit as long as they can "cover it with the flow of money." What this means is that the institution is covering a current (or past) deficit by using the advance payment of monies (tuition) paid for services yet to be rendered. Two or three things need to be said about this maneuver. The first is that it is not an unfamiliar practice in business. The cash flow is not infrequently or inappropriately used to cover an operating deficit. This is a cost-free way to handle a short-term liquidity problem. It is, however, an act of borrowing and should be so noted in order to present an accurate picture of the financial state of the institution. It is, in fact, a borrowing from current funds. Moreover, it is a little like putting a larger fuse in the fuse box if smaller sizes keep getting blown: it masks the fact that there is a problem that needs correction before it becomes a bigger problem, and thus it eliminates an early danger signal. Cash flow does have some elasticity and can be used to stretch a bridge across a temporary chasm; but it is not infinitely elastic and it must reach the limit of its elasticity if the ravine continues to widen. It is dangerous to believe that one need do "nothing" about a deficit.

Federal Aid

An institution can avoid deficits either by reducing expenditures or by seeking additional income. The latter is by far the preferred alternative. One of the major potential sources of new and additional revenue is the federal government.

The type of federal aid preferred by private college and university presidents is facilities grants directly to institutions. They have tried it. They like it. They want more of it. This is, in the most precise sense of the word, a conservative choice. There is some evidence to suggest that it may not be the wisest choice.

The preferred type of federal aid in second place is institutional grants directly to institutions. This is not a conservative choice in the sense of being based upon experience with *federal* aid. It bears, however, an apparent resemblance to other monies that come to an institution to be used at its discretion and doubtless *seems* a conservative choice. There are probably formulas that would make this kind of aid less acceptable than under other formulas, and "strings" that could make it unwelcome; but it is strongly endorsed by private college presidents as a general type of aid.

The next most frequently preferred choice is grants directly to students. This is, again, a type of federal aid with which colleges and universities have had a lot of experience. Most of that experience, to judge by the response of private college presidents, has been good. Such aid has been too little and too inconsistent, but it has demonstrated its value and is a popular choice.

Facilities loans, as distinct from facilities *grants,* is in fourth place.

The type of federal aid fifth most frequently identified as preferred is a federally supported student-loan bank. This is *not* a conservative choice in the sense of being based on experience. It is an idea that has been developing fresh currency as the Carnegie Commission on Higher Education and many individual economists have endorsed some form of this type of aid as part of a balanced program of federal aid. It would, in essence, make available at low interest federally guaranteed loan funds that could be borrowed by individual students to cover their educational costs (including but not limited to tuition) and repaid by them at a rate proportionate to later income.

In sixth place on the preferred list is the category "other loans directly to students."

Seventh most frequently identified as preferred is a proposal that has been around a long time: income tax credit for student expenditures. Many of its proponents are very clear and sometimes single-minded in their espousal of this form of aid. It has, however, a small group of opponents who may feel that not enough is known of its economic effects.

The next two choices are tied for eighth place: interest subsidy and categorical grants to institutions for research and programs. In tenth place is grants to the states for distribution to institutions; in eleventh place, grants to the states for distribution to students.

Although this is the order of preference for various types of federal aid, the magnitude of difference between them— already small—is reduced to insignificant proportions for the leaders when the judgment "acceptable" is joined to "preferred." Facilities grants and loans, institutional grants, grants and loans to students—including a federally supported student-loan bank—are all overwhelmingly endorsed by private colleges and universities. This may suggest that private institutions are so desperate for federal aid that virtually any form could be at least acceptable, even if some forms of it appear preferable.

One respondent may have been speaking for others when he added: "Anything to obtain more funds would at least be acceptable."

Pattern of Plant Indebtedness

Taken collectively, private colleges and universities are in debt for over a quarter (26 per cent) of the book value of their physical plants. In dollars this amounts to over three billion dollars of indebtedness on the physical plant of all private institutions, an average of four million dollars per institution. Over half (51 per cent) of this indebtedness is to the federal government. Slightly under one eighth (12 per cent) of the indebtedness of institutions is to themselves: they have borrowed from their own endowment funds and from their own current funds. Over a quarter of their indebtedness on physical plant is to private sources of funding (26 per cent), 10 per cent to state government, and a minuscule fraction (0.1 per cent) to local government.

How one interprets these figures—the amount of indebtedness and to whom owed—will depend in part on how one views the economic future of these debtors and the degrees of beneficence with which one believes their creditors will act in the event of a declining or failing return on their investment.

Two of the more interesting creditors are the federal government and the institution itself. Relatively few institutions have actually defaulted on federal loans, but several have been forced to ask for some concession—a moratorium on the payment of principal, for example; and some of those in actual default have not recovered their ability to resume debt service payments. The federal government has only difficult choices in these instances.

I have heard of the president of a small private college whose almost fantastic building program in recent years has placed the institution in debt on its physical plant for two thirds of its value and who firmly believes that one day the federal government will forgive all of these outstanding loans. He has since retired and the institution recently hired another president, one committed to the repayment of these loans.

The indebtedness to other institutional funds is also interesting. The institution borrows from itself for the same reasons you and I may pay cash for a purchase rather than buy it on time: we find that we can lend ourselves the money at a cheaper rate than we can borrow it elsewhere. An institution that uses money it could otherwise invest at, say, 5 per cent to save borrowing at 8 per cent nets a clear gain in the transaction; but it has engaged in some incestuous financing that could have very serious implications in the event of further curtailment of income. Being a bad debtor to oneself means that one has already drawn on reserves to which one might turn in a reversal and has no one to sue for recovery. Moreover, the borrowed funds—on which interest is seldom paid—are sterilized as an investment. This sterilization is important in computing the strength of the institution's endowment. One might assume a growth rate and income-earning rate that would improve the endowment and its ability to be used for program functions— but not if it is committed to a noninterest or niggardly-interest loan. The old saw that the man who serves as his own legal advisor has a fool for a client and a dunce for a lawyer may apply with milder force to the institution that borrows from itself too heavily.

Burden of Student Aid

The very large amount of money, an increasing amount of money, being spent on direct student aid places a considerable burden on private higher education and contributes significantly to its deficit condition. Private higher education is caught in an ever widening and more vicious spiral. As it moves to demonstrate its social concern by extending scholarship money to those unable to pay even tuition, it must find revenue to pay for these student-aid expenditures. Typically it has done this, in large part, by raising tuition. In doing so, however, it puts the new tuition charge out of reach for another group of students, who now require subsidy for the difference between last year's cost and this year's. This, in turn, requires further tuition increases, creates still another group needing financial aid, increases the amount of aid needed by the groups previously identified, and so on.

Indirect student aid, arrived at by subtracting tuition and fees from educational and general expenditures (except sponsored research and medical center expenditures), is greater on a per-student basis at the very smallest and the very largest institutions. Institutions enrolling 500 students or less are subsidizing their students' education more highly than any other enrollment group. At over one thousand dollars per student ($1,065) their indirect student aid is 6 per cent more than that of institutions enrolling over 4,000 ($1,001); 41 per cent more than of institutions enrolling between 501 and 1,000 ($633); and well over twice as much as of institutions enrolling between 1,001 and 2,000 ($517) or between 2,001 and 4,000 ($497).

Collective Picture and Individual Institution

Taken collectively, we have said, private higher education carries an indebtedness on its physical plant of over three billion dollars. By the same rough measures of approximation, we can say that in 1968–69 private higher education carried a current-fund indebtedness of over half a billion dollars on a current-fund budget of about five billion dollars. A rough estimate of the total deficit experienced over the years 1967–68 through 1970–71, for all of private higher education, not netted out by combination with surplus years or with institutions running surpluses, would be over $400,000,000.

These deficits are substantial. We live, however, in a nation where the largest railroad requests a federal loan guarantee of $125,000,000 in a deficit situation of more than twice that amount and where the Defense Department seeks $1,400,-000 to stave off bankruptcy for the developer of the C-5A transport plane.

Private higher education, taken as a collective whole, is not yet in desperate straits. Private higher education is not, however, a collective whole. Individual institutions present a wide variety of patterns over these four years. Some march steadily from a surplus or small deficit in 1967–68 into deeper

and deeper deficits. Others have been doing well and continue
to do so. Still others move helter-skelter over the four years
from surplus to deficit or from deficit to surplus and back again.
Indeed, virtually any surplus-deficit pattern possible may be
found to have at least one example.

For institutions running deficits (between 40 and 60 per
cent of all private higher education institutions in a given
year), the financial situation runs from serious to critical. One
quarter of these institutions projected deficits less than 2 per
cent of their current-fund expenditure budgets even in 1970–71.
Another quarter, however, projected deficits in 1969–70 and
1970–71 in excess of 7 per cent. In 1970–71, in fact, the range
of deficit for this group of institutions was from 7.4 per cent to
29.1 per cent of the current-fund budget.

Smaller institutions are particularly vulnerable. Nineteen per cent of those institutions enrolling 500 students or less
are running deficits that are 8 per cent or more of their current-
fund expenditure budgets; 16 per cent of those institutions
enrolling between 500 and 1,000 students are running deficits
of this magnitude; and 8 per cent of those institutions enrolling
between 1,000 and 2,000 are suffering this severely. In contrast,
only 2 per cent of those enrolling between 2,000 and 4,000 and
only 5 per cent of those with more than 4,000 students have
deficits in this range.

Individual institutions simply resist being taken captive
by statistical averages. For this reason, individual institutions,
no matter how perilous their situation as judged by the statistical company they keep, may, like Pauline, be saved from
imminent disaster by the heroic action of a magnificent bequest
or the fortuitous appearance of some other savior or by native
intelligence that enables them to outwit the financial villain
and escape. An individual institution's plight may be favorably
modified by a magnificent gift, by a substantial increase in enrollment, by the favorable effects of legislation imminent in
some states. But statistics take note of the opposite possibilities
as well: the disaffected donor, the declining enrollment, the
inaction or ineffectual action of state legislatures.

Private colleges and universities are apprehensive, and

they have reason to be. Most colleges in the red are staying in the red and many are getting redder, while colleges in the black are generally growing grayer. If the projected deficits are as low as projected, it will be because some very high hopes have been realized on the income side and because many programs have been reduced or eliminated. Taken collectively, these institutions will not long be able to serve higher education and the nation with strength unless *significant* aid is soon forthcoming.

CHAPTER 12

New Approaches
to Finance

Sharvy G. Umbeck

Because the expense side of the budget is receiving attention elsewhere in this volume, I have been asked to confine my comments to matters relating to income. Scrutiny of the history of methods and procedures and policies of college finance over the last century and a half brings into focus radical and profoundly significant shifts. Most private institutions, have always been on the brink of financial disaster. For many institutions, it has been a perpetual environmental condition. Moreover, all colleges and universities, public and private, seem to develop the capacity to spend all the funds they can get. In the earliest years, at most private institutions, modest student fees and even more modest endowment income were augmented by a development program which centered largely around gifts in kind, prayers by the local bishop, and contributed services.

But even though the long-term look brings into focus these dramatic shifts, it is an indisputable fact that changes in the financial policies of colleges have come slowly and painfully. Look, for example, how long it took for the idea of investing endowment funds in dormitory construction to take hold. Or, more directly, how many institutions still follow practices and policies such as the following: they consider classroom buildings, science buildings, libraries to be nonrevenue-producing; they will not build an academic building until all the needed funds are in hand or pledged; they place responsibility for the investment portfolio entirely in the hands of a trustee committee without the benefit of outside professional counsel; they consider all endowment funds completely sacrosanct, whether the funds were placed there by trustee action or by direction of the donor; they consider no portion of stock dividends to be dividend income; they maintain a policy under which a large portion of the endowment portfolio is kept in bonds, on the theory that liquidity of assets will enable the institution to buy common stocks when the market "is right"—and then they hesitate to move into the market at times like November 1970; they are afflicted with a species of "deficit myopia," which focuses attention exclusively on a budget describing a twelve-month operation rather than on a long-term program.

Too many administrators (admittedly their numbers become smaller annually) boast of never having had an operating deficit. It is just possible that they might be leading better institutions if occasionally they had tolerated, or even planned, a deficit. Mind you, I am not suggesting that any college can tolerate deficits over long periods of time. I am simply suggesting that a balance of income and expenditures over a period of three or four or five years might facilitate the development of greater institutional strength than a restricted focus on any one fiscal year. The widespread presence of policies such as those listed above have led me to the conclusion that too many private institutions—usually small and impecunious—have been irreparably harmed by the well-intentioned but generally limited vision of the "small-town banker" who will not loan you money until you can prove you don't need it.

Fortunately, at least among the more progressive and imaginative institutions, significant progress has been made in very recent years. The bold, energetic, and effective actions of TIAA in creating CREF, the challenging research and thought-provoking recommendations of certain distinguished econo-mists, the clout of the Ford Foundation, and the threat of bankruptcy have stimulated increasing numbers of colleges to seek new policies. For example, look at the dramatic change in the definition of endowment income which has evolved in the last four or five years.

But let us look further at the matter of endowment investments. Not all endowment assets are invested in securi-ties. Almost every portfolio includes real estate—real estate of all kinds: farm, desert, urban, improved, and unimproved. When I first came to Knox, I requested a report on each piece of real estate in our portfolio, together with an analysis of its history and its current and potential uses. What a motley assort-ment that was! I vividly recall a report of our chief finance officer regarding some 2,500 acres of land that we held in Loui-siana. His report began in the following encouraging fashion: "I had great difficulty finding land on our property." As you must have surmised, it was swampland. What is more, ulti-mately it proved to be very valuable land. Most of the institu-tions that are blessed with large endowment funds do a good job of searching out the potentials in their diverse real estate holdings. But many smaller institutions handle this potential in an appallingly cavalier fashion. Perhaps there is need for a cooperatively supported management firm, established by a large number of small colleges, which could address itself ex-clusively to exploring opportunities for the development of the diverse real estate holdings of the member colleges. The oppor-tunities inherent in well-located commercial buildings, apart-ment houses, and similar enterprises are readily apparent. The long-range potential of vacant lots, desert acreage, swampland, grazing land, and abandoned factories is not always immedi-ately apparent. For the most flagrant oversight of all, look at the way in which many urban institutions have permitted others to reap the rich benefits of the dramatic real estate appreciation created by campus expansion activities.

Let me turn now to another facet of our income-producing operations: gifts. The vast majority of institutions, public and private alike, are falling far short of their fund-raising potentials. You will note that I have included the public sector. I am well aware of the unpopularity of such a position, but I am convinced that tax-supported colleges and universities can, and should, aggressively seek contributions from individuals, foundations, corporations, and other private sources. A few, too few, public institutions have pursued such programs with conspicuous success. The University of California at Berkeley is the first to come to mind, but there are others. Those who object to such activities by tax-supported institutions are often misled by the false premise that the upper limits of the philanthropic market have been reached and that competition from others will reduce the volume of gifts to the private sector. All available evidence points in precisely the opposite direction. Increased activity by the public sector will, in my studied opinion, increase awareness of and interest in higher education in general, and will enhance the fund-raising productivity of *all* institutions that maintain aggressive, well-directed programs.

With the body of knowledge and skills and arts available today in the area of fund raising, any well-managed institution, possessed of internal vigor and a clear conception of its mission, should be able to put these skills and arts to productive use. The return on investment in this area is superb; at least ten dollars should be produced for every one dollar invested. Still, because of ignorance or lack of vision or sheer inertia, most institutions are plodding along with World War I fund-raising techniques. What is more, a host of charlatans active in the field today, peddling their quack remedies to naïve buyers, have compounded the problem.

On the question of student fees, I shall speak only briefly. Although it is entirely possible that some colleges and universities are pushing the upper limits of what the market will bear by way of pricing policy, I see little reason to abandon my long-held conviction that most colleges have raised tuition too little and too late. If, as most fund raisers agree, it is much easier to obtain gifts for financial aid to students than for the general budget, there seems even more reason for raising tuition rapidly and applying substantial gift funds to financial aid for students who cannot afford to pay the established fees.

As one reviews the spectrum of traditional income sources for higher education—tuition, fees, endowment income, tax appropriations, gifts, and grants—one is struck by the failure of this spectrum to expand. For reasons difficult to comprehend, we have been curiously unimaginative, noninnovative in approaching our income problems. *We must search for viable alternatives.*

As we at Knox developed our long-range plans and addressed ourselves to the question of financing our program in the years ahead, it became inescapably clear that even if we charged the highest tuition we could justify (our tuition is already very high), maximized our endowment return (it is already good), and put as much effort as possible into our fund-raising program (our present development program is quite productive), the cumulative impact of these traditional sources of income still would not be adequate to finance our projected program. The money simply would not be there to do the job. Furthermore, we agreed that it would be neither prudent nor wise to stand by idly and wait for federal or state funds to "bail us out." Such grants, if and when they come, may arrive too late and almost certainly will not be adequate to meet the demands of an effective and significant educational program. It became imperative, therefore, that we undertake a search for new, nontraditional sources of revenue—*in addition to,* not *in replacement of,* traditional income-producing activities. Several alternatives were explored. Through the combined efforts of three very capable trustees, working with an unusually talented vice-president for finance, we projected and implemented a plan for developing additional resources through risk-taking enterprises. As of this date, the list of risk-taking enterprises has expanded to include federal housing projects, real estate subdivisions, an Indian trading post, a motel, a tour operation, a laundry and dry cleaning establishment, and a harness racing track in suburban Chicago.

Incidentally, if any of you think you have problems, I suggest you try running a race track. There is no Manual of

Standard Accounting Practices for race tracks, and do-it-your-self handbooks for the management of harness racing are not exactly flooding the market. As a matter of fact, when I asked a reference librarian what he might have on the subject, he handed me a copy of *Ben Hur*. The care and feeding of eight hundred horses and their grooms and attendants is at least as sensitive a problem as the care and feeding of a faculty. At this particular point in history, the market for manure, like the market for used colleges, is very restricted. Furthermore, our concerns regarding drugs are not confined to the campus. Admittedly, students have come up with some very helpful ideas. As an illustration, they suggest that we adopt a "pass-fail" policy for the race track, instead of "win, place, and show." They claim that "it will relieve tension among the horses."

Most of our enterprises are operated by separate, wholly college-owned, and fully taxed corporations. Present indications suggest that over the next ten years the college will build sub-stantial long-term assets through this mechanism. It is clear, however, that we have not found the ultimate answer. Other new and effective alternatives must and will be explored.

Of course, we would much prefer to confine our energies to the basic tasks of higher education. Given our "druthers," we would not have undertaken this program. I can explain our participation only by likening our situation to that of the gen-tleman who, on the occasion of his seventieth birthday, was asked, "What is it like to be alive at seventy?" The classic reply: "Considering the alternatives, it isn't bad." Well, when Knox College looks down that long, hard, fiscal road ahead, consider-ing the alternatives, being saddled with these extraneous opera-tions isn't bad.

In all candor, this posture is not entirely new at Knox. We like to remind our alumni and friends that our institution was founded in the 1830s by a farmer, a cheesemaker, and a clergyman, who devised and implemented a scheme under which they purchased 36 square miles of midwest prairie land from the government at $1.25 per acre. After setting aside a small—a very small—parcel for the college, they sold the bal-ance of the land to themselves and to others at $5 per acre. The "profit" was utilized to build our first buildings and to establish our first permanent funds. In truth, our entrepreneurial activities have substantial historical precedent.

Now, I am not trying to urge others to emulate or, for that matter, even to approve what we are doing at Knox. I am, however, urging those who represent private institutions to search about for ways and means, other than the time-honored, traditional sources, to assure the funding that future programs will inescapably demand. The job is of such complexity as will demand the combined resourcefulness and imagination of all concerned. The time to start is today, because even today may be too late.

CHAPTER 13

Impact of Admissions on Financial Stability

Dennis L. Johnson

T he challenge of the 1970s may, in the long term, prove to be good for many colleges. Difficult decisions will have to be made in the very near future at hundreds of institutions. With stable enrollment becoming more difficult to achieve, with costs increasing, and with students turning toward less expensive community colleges, a real sense of urgency must be developed at every level of college administration. What, then, is one area that can be changed in the shortest period of time with dramatic results?

The answer may sound too simple—admissions. When private colleges and universities depend on tuition, fees, room and board, and other student charges for from 60 to 90 per cent of their income, they must begin placing greater importance on their admissions effort. The economic impact of even fifty empty beds or classroom chairs echoes through the entire institution—especially the smaller institution, where fifty students may represent one tenth of the total enrollment. Fixed costs such as faculty salaries, plant operation, and needed administrative staff are, by definition, largely irreducible even if income drops appreciably.

Some colleges are operating at deficits of $100,000 to $300,000 per year, and have done so for the last three years. Their creditors will not allow this to continue, their endowment funds are limited or nonexistent, and still some have not set about resolving the problem. At most colleges, a $200,000 deficit can be partially eliminated by good management and approximately one hundred additional students. How, then, does a college president begin the business of enrollment stabilization?

The first step involves a long and critical look at the institution. Who attends? Why? Is the college really worth an extra thousand dollars per semester as compared with a similar program at the local accredited community college? In seeking answers to these questions, the college will begin to learn a great deal about itself and its acceptance by various constituencies. The answers may not be flattering, and sooner or later they will involve individuals. It may be necessary to examine pragmatically every program and the degree of its acceptance by potential students. Unless the college has viable programs meeting the needs of its community, state, church—or any other potential student groups—its future is limited.

The law of supply and demand relating to college admission will not be repealed in the 1970s. The supply of seats available in private colleges—for students with the financial means and the desire to attend—more than matches the demand. Thousands of empty seats are available in hundreds of private colleges, in large part due to the growth of the two-year community college. Unless there is a dramatic change in enrollment trends, private education may enroll no more than about 15 per cent of all college students in 1980.

The competition for freshman students may force four-year colleges to reexamine the purpose and necessity of their freshman and sophomore offerings. Two-year colleges will enroll three out of four freshmen by the end of the present decade, which means that even greater numbers will be seeking transfer to four-year institutions. Yet large numbers of colleges cling to antiquated policies of transfer that drive away two-year graduates. With over 1,100 junior colleges now—and with the Carnegie Commission recommending 200–300 additional ones —four-year colleges and universities will be forced to change. The community colleges will not go away and will continue to prosper. If four-year colleges wish to exist, they must learn to coexist.

Admissions and student recruitment must receive a higher level of priority at most institutions. If one looks only at the economic implications of a successful or failing admissions program, he will see the clear need for greater attention to student recruitment. There must be a real commitment to admissions on the part of all members of the entire college community and this commitment must begin with the president.

Unfortunately, most college presidents know very little about admissions and student recruitment. Perhaps they served on an admissions committee during their climb up the academic ladder to the presidency, but rarely have they been closely involved with admissions. Until recently, admissions was a necessary evil that commanded the president's attention two or three times a year—at budget-planning sessions, at trustee meetings when enrollment was below expectations, and at faculty meetings when the faculty called for better students. The picture has changed, and the president must learn about a new area. The very future of the college hinges on his being able, as chief administrator, to develop an effective admissions program.

Developing an Effective Program

The college president anxious to develop an effective program but in a quandary over where to begin might start by seeking answers to such questions as these:

Do you receive weekly and monthly statistics outlining the number of applications, acceptances, rejections, and deposits? Are enrollment projections soundly based on historical data or on unrealistic optimism?

What is the real cost per student in recruitment of new students? Does the figure include publications, catalogs, and other hidden costs? Do you have data that indicate how this figure is changing?

Does the admissions staff continually look for new sources of well-qualified candidates? Does the staff keep you informed on trends in admissions, new programs used at other institutions, and the interests of the prospective students?

Does the admissions director report directly to you? If not, does his superior have power to support, give immediate decisions, and develop an adequate budget? Is the admissions director and his staff held accountable for every effort and budget expenditure? Do you set performance specifications and insist that they be met?

If admissions personnel do not perform well, are they released? Or is nonperformance rewarded with a new contract and an increase in salary?

Does your faculty understand the importance of admissions and, at the same time, realize the difficult task it has become? Do they offer to assist admissions efforts?

And, most critically, is the admissions officer held in high regard by the academic community on your campus? Is his salary commensurate with his responsibility?

Every type of institution is affected by good management in admissions. Having too many students creates problems for some colleges—nice problems, say the presidents of colleges needing additional students—and these must be managed; but enrollment below projected goals creates more severe fiscal and academic problems: no raises for faculty and staff, no new teaching equipment or facilities, and ill will with creditors.

For these reasons alone the appointment of the admissions director is one of the president's most significant acts. The qualities I consider important in an admissions director—more important than advanced degrees or previous experience, age or sex, or alumni status—are these: a real love for students and their best interests; a desire to convince others that his college is best; a restless ambition to get ahead and move out of admissions in two to four years; an ability to identify with and have empathy for the needs of potential students; an absence of concern for hours worked, days spent, or inconveniences confronted prior to meeting enrollment goals; strong communications and organizational skills; loyalty to his employer; good judgment in evaluating, hiring, training, and, if necessary, terminating employees.

Communications Problem

The admissions problem is exacerbated by a communications problem. Attracting the attention of a media-saturated public is a difficult task today. The present college-age student has grown up with these techniques as part of his life style. Perhaps, therefore, it is time for education to adopt some of the communications methods used by the corporate world.

The low profile of many a college can be seen when its publications are released to the public. Some say that contemporary brochures using color, communications systems adapted from business, and other student-contact programs make an institution look desperate. If they are used in a skillful manner, however, with the best interests of the student uppermost, the student's reaction is positive.

Since the best critics of these descriptive publications are students, it might be a refreshing idea to ask students to design them. There are a number of pragmatic considerations to keep in mind in designing brochures—type of distribution, numbers needed, reprint costs, and the like; but the most important are ones that students have expertise in evaluating: Does it speak to its intended audience? Is it lively and attention-getting? Is the copy simple, clear, and concise? Does it reflect the real institution?

Personal Touch

Even more important than the publications of the college is the ability of the admissions staff to make the institution personal for potential applicants. Through them the applicants can see an institution that really cares. It is an appalling fact that the "personalized" education small colleges claim is rarely mirrored by the admissions effort. Potential students who generate their own applications are frequently treated with no more individual concern than names drawn from a general list —even though students who initiate interest are the best leads a college has. In an effective admissions office, the director spends as much time assisting the rejected student in finding another college as he does in encouraging the very able student to attend his own institution. Colleges must treat all candidates with greater warmth and concern if they are, in fact, going to keep the students' interest.

Sources for More Students

There are many potential sources for more students, but admissions policies may have to be adjusted to develop them. For example, approximately one million men will be leaving military service in the next year. About 78 per cent of them have a high school diploma, or the equivalent, *and* government benefits. Yet far too few colleges have made a concentrated effort to attract veterans or have considered realistic admissions policies for them. Disabled Vietnam veterans come with special problems, but they have extra financial benefits that make college attendance a real possibility. The new PREP and tutorial programs give a college an opportunity to reach out and be reached.

Nearly 400,000 students left college last year for academic reasons; yet these young people were supposedly among the best qualified of high school graduates. The whole college decision process leads me to believe that a high percentage of these students made a wrong initial choice. Some students and their parents spend more time in purchasing an automobile than in making the critical decision on which college to attend. Many of these students are still well qualified for college. Their wrong initial choice ought not prevent them from a second chance.

Church-related colleges should assume a greater identification with their native constituencies while at the same time showing college-age students that the institution has a uniqueness and flavor consonant with the 1970s. The old tired phrases still used in college publications no longer speak to the needs and interests of this generation. Students are looking for certain fresh qualities and will respond to the institutions that meet their interests.

The 1970s will be a decade of change for colleges and for college admissions. The secret of the successful institution will be whether it manages change or is managed by change.

CHAPTER 14

Does Private Education Have a Future?

Howard R. Bowen

Like most of you I have faced student unrest; I have absorbed the angry criticisms of alumni, parents, and public leaders; I have watched faithful donors withdraw their support; I have faced the outcries of faculty when budgets were cut; and I have witnessed the apparent callousness with which federal and state officials have rebuffed legitimate requests for financial aid and have found political advantage in abusing the colleges. I have often wondered whether our colleges and universities can survive as a vital and effective force in our society. But when I consider the matter, I always end up with the conclusion that they will survive because they are urgently needed and because the means to their survival clearly exist.

We educators have been buffeted in the past few years. We are on the defensive and off balance. But I believe the time has come for us to stop commiserating and apologizing and to go on the offensive. As a group we have turned in a good performance. The colleges and universities of this country are better academic institutions than they have ever been. We have little to apologize for—even including campus unrest, which on the whole we have handled with considerable skill and sensitivity.

I am the first to admit that orderly change—perhaps radical change—is called for, as our colleges and universities adjust to the needs of the last quarter of the twentieth century. The traditional pattern does not altogether fit a new and different era, a different mood, different social problems, different classes of society, and different aspirations. There is a kind of social revolution in the air, and we are inevitably and properly affected by it. But to admit the need for change is to accept a welcome challenge, not to call for us to go on the defensive.

Indispensability of Higher Education

The basic reason that I am optimistic about the future of higher education is that our colleges and universities are indispensable. Our society could not survive, let alone prosper, without them. Learning is the principal and basic resource of our society. Virtually all aspects of our life—our economy, the education of our children, our health and welfare, our law enforcement, our recreation, the arts, our national defense—depend on large numbers of highly educated persons and on learning derived from basic research and scholarship. Moreover, the many problems that plague us today—war, poverty, racial tension, urban blight, pollution, and materialism—can be solved only if we have enlightened leadership, a broadly educated populace, and a large cadre of skilled professional and technical workers.

It is also evident that in the years ahead our consumption will or should be directed increasingly to services and to cultural activities, and relatively less to goods of the kind that flow from industrial assembly lines. The service industries already account for more than half of the GNP, and by 1980 more than half of all our workers will be engaged in white-collar jobs.[1] In the next generation we shall be seekers of quality of life rather than quantity of things. To accomplish these shifts, both producers and consumers will require higher levels of education and more profound insights into the good life.

The public knows all these things subconsciously. Indeed the reason that the problems of the campus are so traumatic is precisely that the public perceives that learning is the foundation of our society and the principal means to the solution of our many vexing problems. The lapse from popular support of higher education is bound to be temporary, *provided* educators can discern future societal needs for higher education in the last quarter of the twentieth century and adjust accordingly.

That the public clearly recognizes the value of higher education is evidenced by the ever larger numbers of young people who are attending. There is no evidence that parents, even those most vocally critical, are discouraging their children from going to college. I also believe, though I have no statistical evidence, that the public is becoming more understanding of the contemporary student generation. I am finding much more appreciation of the role of students and other young people as critics in bringing into focus the nagging social problems and injustices of our time. In my opinion, we can look with some pride on the fact that our young people, the products of our higher education, have helped to show America the fallacies and mistakes in its values and in its policies and have helped to extend the American heritage of liberty, justice, and idealism.

Case for Private Higher Education

So far I have been speaking of higher education generally. The rest of my remarks will be directed toward *private* higher education, which appears to be under especially crush-

[1] Conference Board, *Guide to Consumer Markets, 1970,* as quoted in *Los Angeles Times,* December 21, 1970, p. 1.

ing financial pressures these days. Many informed people seriously predict the demise of most independent institutions and expect them to be absorbed into the public systems or to go the way of the private preparatory academy.

The case for numerous and strong private colleges or universities is in my judgment compelling, though it is not widely understood. The alternative would be higher education as a monolithic public enterprise. Such a system of higher education would be managed by absentee state boards and central state bureaucracies. They would be heavily influenced by Washington, they would be readily susceptible to politics, and they would often be marred by impersonality and uniformity. The role of the private sector is to provide *diversity* and *leadership* and in so doing to serve the public sector of higher education as well as the society at large.

The private college or university contributes to *diversity* when it offers differentiated styles of education suited to particular clienteles. A private college contributes by serving a particular area, a particular vocation, a particular ethnic or religious group. It may offer small, personalized community life; it may appeal to those who place importance on the transmission of values through higher education; it may cater to those of exceptional ability or, alternatively, to those of low ability; it may offer unusual methods of instruction; it may provide opportunities for off-campus study or social service; it may appeal to adult learners. Through the diversity offered by private institutions, the higher educational system can serve the needs of more people and offer more choices to students and their parents than would be possible, or at least likely, in a public system of higher education.

In their *leadership* role, private colleges and universities are responsible for demonstrating the nature of academic excellence, setting academic standards, keeping alive and flourishing the ideal of liberal learning, presenting a living example of academic freedom, and being innovative and experimental. In the realm of leadership, their mission is to use the independence and flexibility that comes with privacy to set the example of what a college should be like. In practice, the entire academic community has looked to the top private institutions—large and small—for leadership, and their example has been a major factor in the freedom and advancement of the public sector.

I am sorry to say, however, that not every private college contributes to diversity or leadership. Those that offer only conventional programs and thus contribute nothing meaningful to diversity, and those with little to offer in the way of useful leadership, are the colleges that will in the long run be threatened with extinction. I do not mean that all such institutions will succumb, but the road ahead for them is rough and rocky.

If a college's academic program and campus environment are in no way distinctive, and if it fails to serve as an influential example to other institutions, it has little to offer students and little to attract donors. The only thing that can be said for it is that it will draw nearby students who find it less costly or more convenient than the distant state university, and that it will save money for the taxpayers, since it will bear some of the costs that the state institutions would otherwise have to assume. From the social point of view, however, the cost is there, and is borne by people in their role as students and donors rather than in their role as taxpayers. Such an institution is no asset to the private system of higher education, because it will attract some donors who would otherwise support more worthy private institutions.

On the other hand, private colleges and universities that offer meaningful diversity and effective leadership have a solid base, can attract both students and donors, and can make a significant contribution to American higher education and American society. It is incumbent on every private institution to take stock of itself and to plan its program and its campus environment so that it can contribute to diversity and leadership in terms of the societal needs of the next quarter century. Such planning is especially required at this time, when higher education is entering new and uncharted territory. The future success of any private college will depend on its ability to discern future needs in the content and form of higher education and to shape its program to meet those needs. The responsibility of private institutions is especially compelling because they have—or should have—the independence and flexibility to blaze new trails. If they fail, private higher education will die and our nation will have lost a vital source of diversity and leadership. If they succeed, private colleges and universities will flourish and become harbingers of a renewed society.

Financial Crisis

We can assert with some confidence that the American people could, if they chose, provide enough money for good higher education, even in a year of low stock prices and declining economic activity. The higher education industry, public and private, absorbs between 1 or 2 per cent of the GNP, and discretionary income is ample to cover reasonable increases in this percentage. The problem is therefore not financial or economic; it is a matter of public and private priorities.

Also, the present financial crisis is by no means the first one in the history of American higher education. Private higher education did, in fact, survive the Great Depression, World War II, and the early 1950s after the departure of the GIs. Indeed, I cannot remember a time when one could be sure where the money was coming from next year, let alone five or ten years hence. In fact, except for the last year or two, I have been continually astonished that my wildest expectations have not only been realized but even surpassed. I have faith that our private colleges will survive the present crisis, primarily because the private sector is so valuable a part of our social fabric that the nation cannot afford to let it die.

The crisis is a relative matter in that it affects rich as well as poor institutions. Yale, Princeton, and Stanford feel the pinch along with institutions of the most modest means. The explanation, of course, is that the budget of any institution is determined not by some absolute standard of need but by the amount of money it has been able to raise. The law of academic budgeting is very simple. It is that an institution will raise all the money it can, and it will spend all the money it raises. The cost per student in any institution is a function of customary income, not necessarily of educational need. Deficits, when they occur, represent a gap between the accustomed institutional standard of living and income—not necessarily a gap between the amount needed for good education and income. However, all colleges are locked into heavy fixed costs (including faculty tenure) and lack the capacity to adjust quickly.

Hence, no matter how rich the institution, to cope with a deficit is hard and slow. Moreover, each institution rightly tries to protect its hard-won position and to resist retrenchment and retrogression. In no institution that I know of, regardless of wealth, does the board, president, or faculty feel that they are wasting large sums of money and could reduce expenditures without serious loss to both institutional and social values. But the problem is clearly more devastating for financially poor institutions than for rich ones.

A deficit can be overcome either by raising income or by cutting expenditures. But the matter is complicated by the fact that income and expenditures are not independent variables. Donors, even including governments, like to give to new and interesting projects and to progressing institutions. Few want to back a loser or to give money just to meet a deficit. Students like to attend and pay tuitions to vigorous and exciting institutions which offer the amenities, not to retrenching and penurious colleges.

Hence, there are risks either in a policy of retrenchment or in a policy of increasing income. Retrenchment, because of its adverse effect on income, may in the end fail to bring about a balanced budget. On the other hand, a policy of maintaining or increasing expenditures may not produce the hoped-for effect on income and may end up in unmanageable deficits. Prudence probably requires in most cases a selective combination of retrenchment and advancement. But it is clear that mere belt-tightening may not in the end solve the problem. It may only end in death by starvation. There may be institutions in which the better gamble is to play for increased income. By that device, at least, the institution makes educational progress in the short run. If it dies, it dies with honor, not ignominy.

Policies for Meeting Financial Crisis

The first policy for the private college, in my opinion, is not to panic. The hard-won gains of the past fifteen years should not be sold out by precipitous retrenchment. Some time will be required to make necessary adjustments to new conditions, and we should if possible hold things together during that turn-around time.

The second is to make interesting plans for the inter-mediate and long-run future, plans of the kind that will attract support and reassure donors. Donors who must bail out the colleges must be made to feel that the ship will float and eventually go on to new successes. I can hardly overstress the importance of sound long-range planning in meeting the imme-diate crisis. A sense of looking ahead with vision and confidence and realism is needed to win financial support and also to strengthen internal institutional morale.

Third, we should not be too quick to abandon our tradi-tional mode of finance. The private colleges are private because they have been financed primarily by tuitions and philan-thropy. They have been socially useful because they have held tuitions to reasonable levels and have accepted students from a wide spectrum of social classes. Private colleges should con-tinue to rely heavily on private philanthropy as the only secure way to retain independence on terms that will enable them to carry out their mission.

Regarding tuition, private colleges should not give way to the deceptively attractive doctrine that the full cost of higher education should be shifted to students by means of high tuitions combined with various schemes for putting students into debt. Private higher education produces enormous social benefits and should be widely available at reasonable cost. Also, private educators should not press for high tuitions in state institutions as a way of improving the competitive position of the private sector. The many proposals for shifting the costs to students are antisocial at a time in our history when oppor-tunity must be opened up in diverse institutions to millions of minority and poor people on the same terms as they were opened up to you and me a generation ago.

In my judgment, a reasonable policy would be for tuition to cover no more than half to two thirds of educational cost and for it to increase from year to year only in proportion to increases in average family income, or perhaps 3 or 4 per cent a year on the average. To go the route of full-cost tuition would make the private colleges indistinguishable from proprietary institutions and would cost them their independence just as surely as absorption by government would. The assumption underlying these remarks on tuition is that private gifts must continue to be a mainstay of private college finance—with all the fund-raising effort that this statement implies. It would be a great mistake to create the impression among donors that a new system of finance that will not require their gifts is just around the corner.

Fourth, we must of course slow down the rate of increase in expenditures per student. During the boom period from 1955 to 1969, educational and general expenditures *per student* increased by nearly 6 per cent a year. In the next few years this rate will have to fall sharply. There can be no indefinite continuation of automatic salary increases of 6 or 7 per cent a year, and there can be few new programs and amenities. Many institutions will get along with little or no increases and with introducing only those new programs that can be funded by improvements in efficiency or by cutting out low-priority activities. This will not be all bad. Any organization can benefit from reappraisal of its spending and from cutbacks. However, the slowing of the pace of advancement will be hard on those colleges that have never had enough resources to do an acceptable educational job.

A special comment on faculty and staff salaries: Salaries in the early 1950s were disgraceful and inadequate to attract and hold capable people in college teaching. With help from many sources, presidents and boards everywhere willingly pushed for salary increases. For many years now, the increases have averaged 6 to 7 per cent a year. In the process, the economic status of the professor has advanced dramatically, and a great deal of talent has been drawn into the profession—to the extent that we now fear a surplus of Ph.D.s. Clearly, routine salary increases of 6 or 7 per cent are not going to be needed in the next few years to attract and hold adequate faculties. However, we seem to have got caught up in a kind of salary contest in which we measure institutional prestige and self-respect by AAUP salary ratings. We have accustomed our faculties and staffs to the idea that anything less than a 6 or 7 per cent increase is tantamount to a cut.

The time has come, I think, to give attention to priorities other than faculty salaries. The colleges must end their role as the automatic conduit by which the proceeds of annual tuition increases are transmitted to faculty in the form of higher salaries. Higher priority must now be accorded to stopping the escalation of tuitions and meeting other institutional needs, rather than going on with the now customary faculty salary increases. In the long run, annual salary increases averaging 3 or 4 per cent, corresponding to the rise in general economic productivity, may prove to be adequate.

Fifth, attention should be given to improvements in efficiency. Private business is often able to offset increases in wages and other costs by efficiency gains, with the result that product prices can be held steady or even fall. In the past, higher education has made some efficiency gains but in all candor they have been minuscule. Education is confronted with the same problem as other labor-intensive service industries like architecture, health care, or barber service—all of which exhibit the same rising costs as education. Nevertheless, some things can be done, and educators have a heavy obligation to cut costs when possible without unduly sacrificing quality.

Among possible ways are eliminating monumental architecture and substituting short-term structures; using low-cost personnel to assist expensive professionals; extending independent study; adopting the Ruml Plan of providing some instruction in large lectures; using teaching machines when they are appropriate; simplifying the curriculum—for instance, by avoiding unnecessary duplication among neighboring institutions; weeding out unnecessary or extraneous or high-cost activities such as esoteric language programs, adult education efforts, intercollegiate athletics, outmoded student advisory services, specialized teacher-education programs, and others that you will all think of. As Professor Gordon Douglass and I have shown, feasible economies in instruction can be substantial.[2] However, these economies can be achieved only if the institution is willing to add to its enrollment without adding to its staff, or is willing to reduce the size of its staff.

The problem of reducing staff at a time when reemployment opportunities are slack raises serious practical and ethical problems. I personally believe society would be better off if our faculties could be kept intact. They perform important scholarly, research, and service functions as well as teaching functions, and it is by no means self-evident that what is called efficiency in instruction would also result in social efficiency in the long run.

Sixth, some review of endowment policy may be needed. For those institutions without endowment this thought may be a bit ironic. The Ford Foundation has issued a report advocating aggressive investment policies to increase the long-term yield. Another proposal is to raise the rate of realized return on endowment from the typical 5 per cent to perhaps 8 per cent, to reflect more adequately the average long-term yield on stocks when capital gains are included. Many trust and pension funds are raising the realized rate of return in this manner. At Claremont Graduate School, this change alone would convert a sizable deficit into a large surplus.

Another possibility would be to adopt the concept of term endowment. At present, most institutions accept current gifts for immediate spending and accept endowments that are held in perpetuity, but few regularly take gifts in which the principal and income may be spent over a term such as fifteen years. By allowing the corpus as well as income to be spent, an institution can greatly increase the yield of an endowment; at the same time, financial stability and continuity are achieved,

---

[2] Howard Bowen and Gordon Douglass, *Efficiency in Liberal Education* (New York: McGraw-Hill, 1971).

since the endowment is available over a period of years. For example, one million dollars invested at 4¼ per cent over a fifteen year period under this plan would yield a yearly sum of $96,000 for a total of $1,442,000.

Role of Government

Government also has a critical place in the future of private higher education. I am going to describe what I think that role should be in six simple propositions.

1. Government should continue to provide full tax exemption for legitimate gifts to private higher education and for the legitimate educational activities of colleges and universities. While no one wishes college finance to be a vehicle for tax avoidance or evasion, tax exemption provides a defensible and solid foundation for the financing and the independence of private institutions.

2. Government should take over the entire cost of student aid on terms that would allow for tuition differences between students attending public institutions and those attending private institutions. Student aid now constitutes as much as 10 to 15 per cent of the total budgets of many private colleges and is rapidly rising as minority students are attending in ever larger numbers. This one item in the budget accounts for more than the entire deficit of most private institutions. If government were to take over this burden and were to provide differential aid to students in private colleges, these institutions would attract large numbers of students of all classes and their critical financial problems would be solved. At the same time, taxpayers would be relieved of the burden of educating many students who could afford to attend private rather than public institutions.

3. Government should take over the costs of special services needed to help minority and other disadvantaged students to attend, adjust to, and graduate from private colleges. These costs could be paid as a special institutional allowance accompanying student aid to eligible students, along lines recommended in the Rivlin and Kerr reports.

4. Government should provide a substantial portion of capital costs for private colleges through grants, not loans.

5. Government should provide modest unrestricted grants for general operations, based on simple and objective formulas.

6. All these proposals should be effectuated in such a way that private colleges would have incentives to keep tuitions within reasonable bounds and private donors would have incentives to give generously. A danger of government aid is that it might merely replace support from private donors.

I have purposedly refrained from elaborating these recommendations in detail. I have not even suggested a division of labor between federal and state governments. I offer these recommendations as illustrative of a set of proposals that might be advocated by the entire private higher educational community of this country.

What I really hope—and this is my main message—is that private educators will construct a nationally agreed-upon program for government participation in the financing of private colleges and universities and will work together to get this program adopted, using every known device of public relations and political action. The private colleges represent an indispensable part of American life that is in danger of liquidation; they face problems of unprecedented severity. But there are workable solutions. And so I ask that the private institutions band together to formulate a concrete plan for useful governmental support and to work toward its adoption. Foundation support would be helpful in carrying out some parts of this plan.

What I have in mind is that AAC, perhaps in concert with other national organizations such as CFAE and ICFA, should give leadership in organizing the private colleges. The effort would have three purposes: to formulate a concrete and uncomplicated legislative program for both federal and state governments; to carry out a major national information program about private higher education—in order to lay the groundwork for the legislative program and also to give support to the ongoing private fund raising of the individual colleges;

to mount a major political effort in Washington and in every state capital to bring about enactment of needed legislation.

I am thinking of a program that would extend over several years and would cost millions. At least as much money should be devoted to securing the place of private higher education in our society as is allotted to selling Ivory soap or Buick cars. The program would make use of all the media and it would focus on particular agreed-upon objectives. The purpose would be to establish in the American consciousness the idea that private higher education is important, to show how private support reinforced by selective public support could make private higher education secure and strong, to back up institutional fund raising, and to push through Congress and the state assemblies the necessary legislation.

Such a program should in no way become an attack upon or a threat to the public institutions. It should be based on the premise that the public and private sectors are complementary and mutually supportive. The difficulty is that the private sector seldom speaks with one voice about its distinctive contributions or about its problems and needs. It is time that the private college story be told by an authentic and effective voice.

Index